THE

ROCKING

BOOK OF

ROCKS

WIDE EYED EDITIONS

CONTENTS

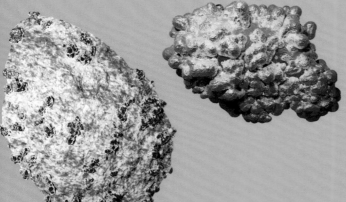

INTRODUCTION

Rocks are all around us, from explosive volcanoes, magnificent mountains, and sandy deserts, to muddy sea floors, winding river valleys, and even asteroids in outer space! If you take away the thin surface layer of soils and the sprinkling of water that makes up the oceans, you're left with—you guessed it—rock!

And rocks aren't just in the landscapes around us. Computers, smartphones, medicines, buildings, airplanes, and even space shuttles are all made from rocks and MINERALS.

Understanding how rocks form helps us to understand how the Earth and the solar system work. Rocks can teach us about how the Earth has changed over millions of years and what it might look like in the future.

The study of rocks and minerals is called GEOLOGY, and the scientists that study them are called GEOLOGISTS. This book will give you all you need to understand just how important rocks are. It might even help you to become a future geologist!

DID YOU KNOW?
Geologists study everything from volcanoes, earthquakes, and the way the Earth works, to the start of life on Earth and ancient creatures like dinosaurs and PREHISTORIC sharks.

DID YOU KNOW?
You can find definitions for any of the words in CAPITAL LETTERS at the back of this book in the glossary. Head to page 94 if you are unsure about the meaning of these words.

WHAT IS A ROCK?

So, let's start at the beginning. What exactly is a rock? We've all seen them and touched them, but what are they? Well, a rock is a naturally occurring solid that is formed from MINERALS or ORGANIC materials (like ancient plants and trees).

Rocks are put into groups according to how they form. There are three main types of rock: igneous, sedimentary, and metamorphic. This book will look at how and where these different types of rocks form and tell you all you need to know to identify them.

WHAT IS A MINERAL?

Minerals are the building blocks of rocks. They are naturally occurring solids, which means they have not been made by humans. Minerals are also INORGANIC, so not made from living things like plants and animals. They are made from mixtures of CHEMICAL ELEMENTS like oxygen, silicon, and IRON. Every mineral has its own set of chemical elements arranged in a particular structure.

Minerals mix together to form rocks. Some rocks are made from just one mineral, but most of them are made from a combination of different minerals. Identifying minerals helps us to figure out what type of rock we are looking at and how it might have formed.

THE STRUCTURE OF THE EARTH

Walking on the surface of the Earth, you might have no idea of the scorching temperatures and the churning and swirling of molten rocks going on thousands of miles below your feet. Let's take a closer look at all that activity going on deep beneath the surface!

At the center of the Earth, a whopping 4,000 miles below your feet, is the solid **inner core**, mostly made up of iron and NICKEL (metal). This is the hottest part of the Earth at a sizzling 9,000–12,500°F: that's the same temperature as the surface of the sun!

Next we have the **outer core**, between 3,200 and 1,800 miles below your feet, which is liquid rock, also made from iron and nickel.

Then we get to the **mantle**. The mantle takes up an enormous 85% of the planet! It spans from 1,800 miles depth right up to the start of the crust, at around 25 miles depth and varies between 1,800 and 6,700°F. The mantle is solid rock, but in some places, usually at plate boundaries, temperatures and pressures can cause the rock to melt. This creates molten magma that can make its way up to the surface and erupt out of volcanoes as red-hot lava.

TECTONIC PLATES

The surface of the Earth might look like one continuous layer, but it is actually broken up into different pieces. These pieces are called tectonic plates, and they fit together like a jigsaw puzzle. You won't be able to feel it, but the Earth's tectonic plates are constantly moving very, very slowly. It is where these different plates meet that lots of volcanic and earthquake activity happens!

The areas where plates meet are called plate boundaries. In some places, the plates are moving apart; in other places, they are rubbing alongside each other; and in other areas, they are colliding very slowly. It's along these boundaries that weave across the Earth's surface where we find magma rising to the surface and the formation of volcanoes and giant mountains. This formation is all down to the movement of tectonic plates on the Earth's surface.

TECTONIC PLATES are cool slabs of rock made from the Earth's crust as well as some of the Earth's upper mantle. They slide over the hotter mantle in the interior of the Earth, by a process not yet fully understood. Over time, they get thicker until the weight of the slab causes it to sink back down into the Earth's interior, slowly pulling the rest of the plate with it. This sinking happens along colliding plate boundaries called *subduction zones*, which can be found all around the edges of the Pacific Ocean.

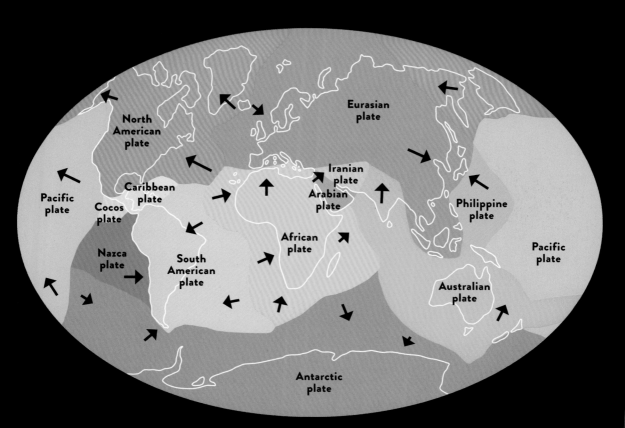

North American plate

Eurasian plate

Caribbean plate

Iranian plate

Arabian plate

Philippine plate

Pacific plate

Cocos plate

Nazca plate

South American plate

African plate

Pacific plate

Australian plate

Antarctic plate

GEOLOGICAL TIMELINE

The Earth is an incredible 4.5 billion years old. If you imagined all of this time as a full 24-hour day, humans wouldn't appear until the last two minutes! On this page, we're going to learn about some of the major geological events that have shaped our planet. Let's take a closer look.

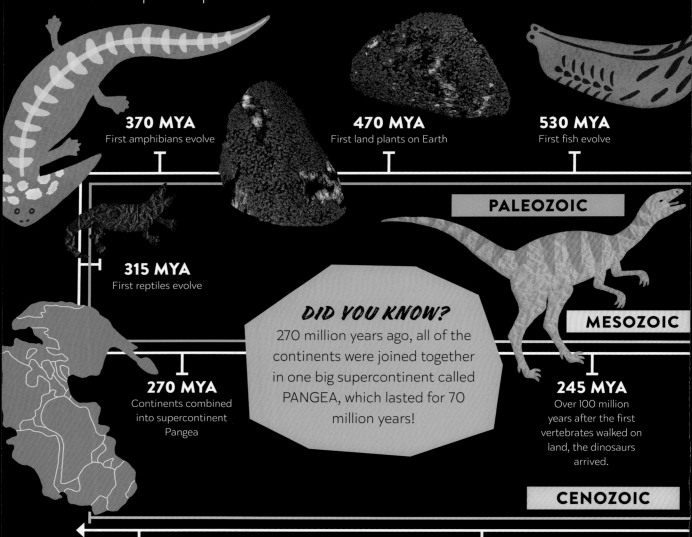

370 MYA
First amphibians evolve

470 MYA
First land plants on Earth

530 MYA
First fish evolve

PALEOZOIC

315 MYA
First reptiles evolve

270 MYA
Continents combined into supercontinent Pangea

DID YOU KNOW?
270 million years ago, all of the continents were joined together in one big supercontinent called PANGEA, which lasted for 70 million years!

MESOZOIC

245 MYA
Over 100 million years after the first vertebrates walked on land, the dinosaurs arrived.

CENOZOIC

TODAY
An INTERGLACIAL period (the warm period) between two ice ages. The next glacial period could be thousands of years or tens of thousands of years away.

2.6 MYA
Ice Ages. Over the last 2.6 million years, the Earth has been through a series of ice ages where large parts of the Earth have been covered in massive ice sheets and glaciers.

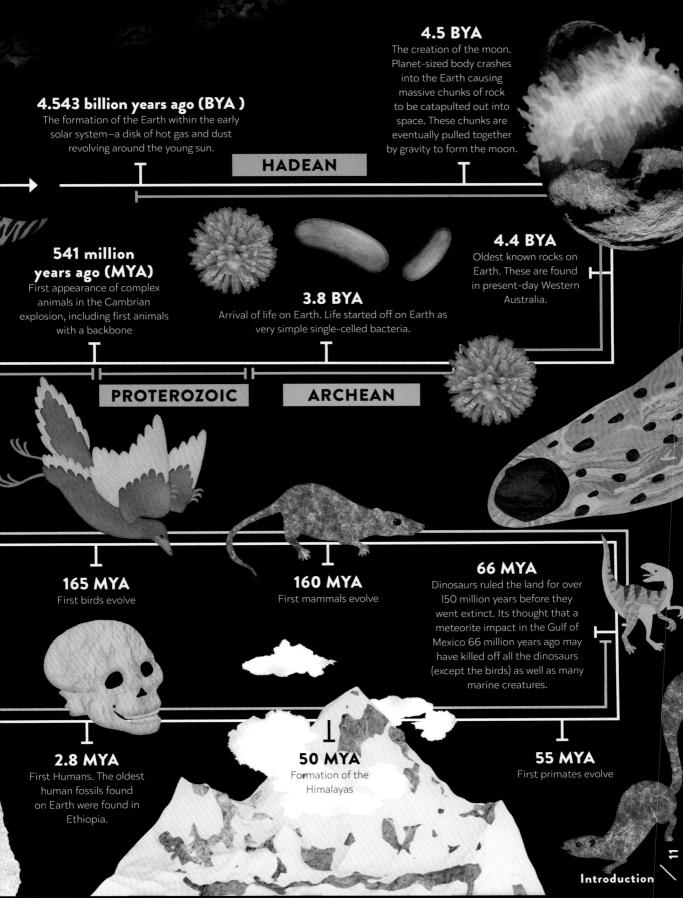

4.543 billion years ago (BYA)
The formation of the Earth within the early solar system—a disk of hot gas and dust revolving around the young sun.

4.5 BYA
The creation of the moon. Planet-sized body crashes into the Earth causing massive chunks of rock to be catapulted out into space. These chunks are eventually pulled together by gravity to form the moon.

HADEAN

541 million years ago (MYA)
First appearance of complex animals in the Cambrian explosion, including first animals with a backbone

3.8 BYA
Arrival of life on Earth. Life started off on Earth as very simple single-celled bacteria.

4.4 BYA
Oldest known rocks on Earth. These are found in present-day Western Australia.

PROTEROZOIC

ARCHEAN

165 MYA
First birds evolve

160 MYA
First mammals evolve

66 MYA
Dinosaurs ruled the land for over 150 million years before they went extinct. Its thought that a meteorite impact in the Gulf of Mexico 66 million years ago may have killed off all the dinosaurs (except the birds) as well as many marine creatures.

2.8 MYA
First Humans. The oldest human fossils found on Earth were found in Ethiopia.

50 MYA
Formation of the Himalayas

55 MYA
First primates evolve

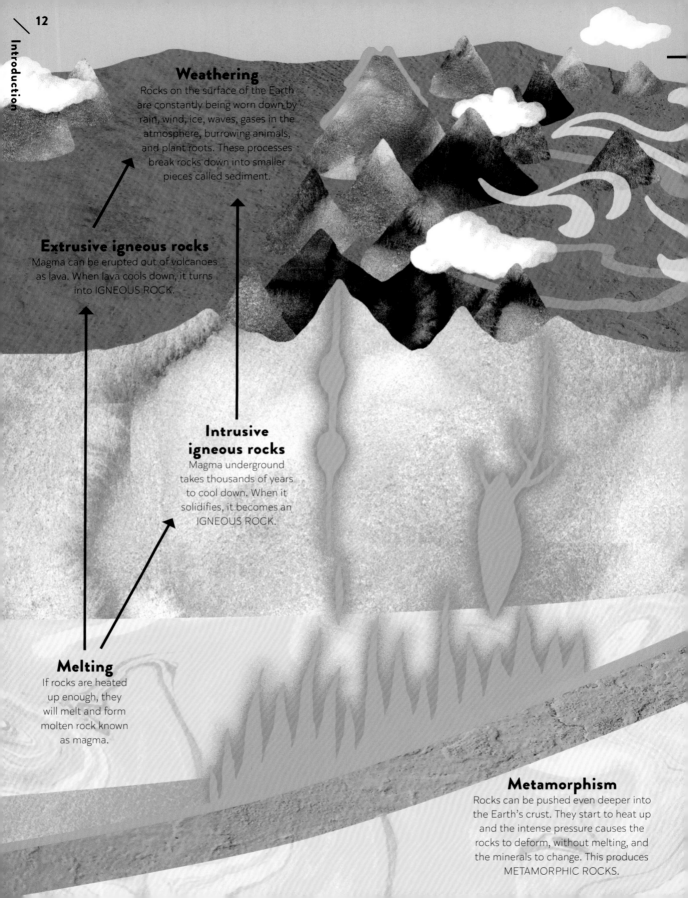

Weathering

Rocks on the surface of the Earth are constantly being worn down by rain, wind, ice, waves, gases in the atmosphere, burrowing animals, and plant roots. These processes break rocks down into smaller pieces called sediment.

Extrusive igneous rocks

Magma can be erupted out of volcanoes as lava. When lava cools down, it turns into IGNEOUS ROCK.

Intrusive igneous rocks

Magma underground takes thousands of years to cool down. When it solidifies, it becomes an IGNEOUS ROCK.

Melting

If rocks are heated up enough, they will melt and form molten rock known as magma.

Metamorphism

Rocks can be pushed even deeper into the Earth's crust. They start to heat up and the intense pressure causes the rocks to deform, without melting, and the minerals to change. This produces METAMORPHIC ROCKS.

Erosion

Sediment such as sand, mud, and pebbles is carried away by rivers, winds, and glaciers.

Deposition

Sediment is dumped in low-energy environments such as seas, beaches, and lakes.

Burial

Over thousands of years, sediment builds up into layers. These layers are then buried deeper and deeper beneath the Earth's surface. Eventually the pressure squeezes the sediment so much it becomes a SEDIMENTARY ROCK.

Uplift

Rocks that form deep in the Earth's crust can be forced up to the surface. This happens when tectonic plates collide and push up huge mountain belts.

THE ROCK CYCLE

Over thousands and millions of years, rocks can be moved around, broken down, and completely transformed into new rocks. They can be carried away by rivers and glaciers, deposited in new places, melted under extreme heat, and deformed under immense pressure deep within the Earth's crust, only to be uplifted again to the surface. All of these processes are part of the rock cycle, and it means that all rocks on Earth are very slowly changing from one rock type to another! Let's take a closer look.

WHAT IS AN IGNEOUS ROCK?

IGNEOUS ROCKS are one of the three main rocks in the rock cycle. They are made when molten rock from deep within the Earth cools to form solid rock. If you look closely, you will see that most igneous rocks are made from jumbled-up mixtures of crystals that are stuck together. These crystals are different igneous minerals. They can be lots of different colors and sizes, but where do they come from?

Billions of years ago, in the early solar system, lumps of rock orbiting around the Sun smashed together to form the Earth. These impacts were so violent that they generated huge amounts of heat, causing the Earth's surface to be completely molten. Over time, this molten surface cooled down to form the Earth's rocky crust, made from igneous rock.

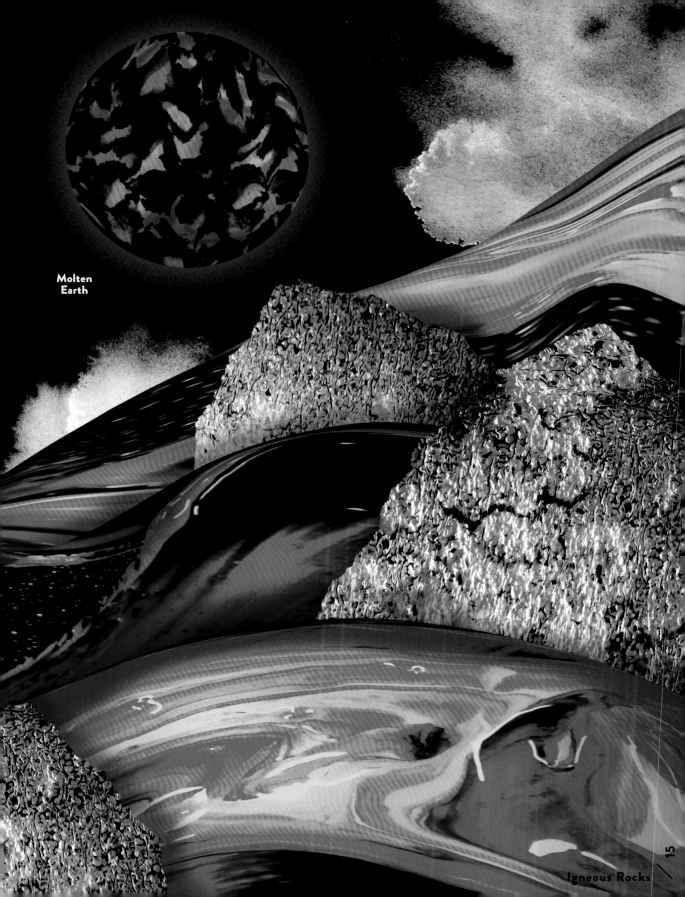

Molten
Earth

Igneous Rocks

WHERE DO IGNEOUS ROCKS FORM?

Igneous rocks are grouped according to where they form on Earth. They can be either intrusive or extrusive.

INTRUSIVE IGNEOUS ROCKS

Intrusive igneous rocks form from magma deep within the Earth's crust and MANTLE. Some of this magma may erupt through volcanoes on the Earth's surface, but most of it gets trapped inside the crust. Here it collects in huge pools called magma chambers. It is much, much hotter deep inside the Earth's crust than it is on the surface. Intrusive rocks therefore take thousands or even millions of years to cool down before they become solid rock.

CRY
FOR

Liqu
magr

Growing crystals

Intergrown crystals

DID YOU KNOW?

Extrusive rocks are also known as volcanic rocks, named after Vulcan, the Roman god of fire, and intrusive rocks can be known as plutonic rocks, named after Pluto, the Roman god of the underworld.

EXTRUSIVE IGNEOUS ROCKS

When volcanoes erupt hot LAVA onto the Earth's surface, it cools down very quickly and hardens into rock, sometimes only taking a few minutes. Lava cools down quickly because the Earth's surface is so much colder than the molten lava, which can be hotter than 2,200°F!

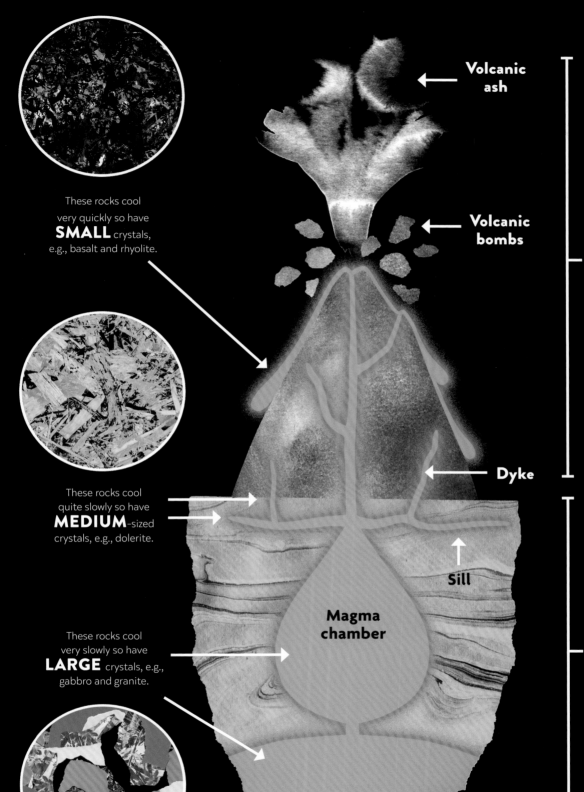

Volcanic ash

Volcanic bombs

These rocks cool very quickly so have **SMALL** crystals, e.g., basalt and rhyolite.

Dyke

These rocks cool quite slowly so have **MEDIUM**-sized crystals, e.g., dolerite.

Sill

Magma chamber

These rocks cool very slowly so have **LARGE** crystals, e.g., gabbro and granite.

INTRUSIVE IGNEOUS ROCKS

There are lots of different types of intrusive igneous rock. They all form below the Earth's surface and usually have large, well-formed CRYSTALS. Here are some examples.

Plagioclase feldspar (white)

Potassium feldspar (pink)

Granite

Granite is one of the best-known intrusive igneous rocks. It forms in magma chambers and large structures within the Earth's crust. Granite is mostly white, gray, or pink in color.

Quartz (transparent)

Biotite (black)

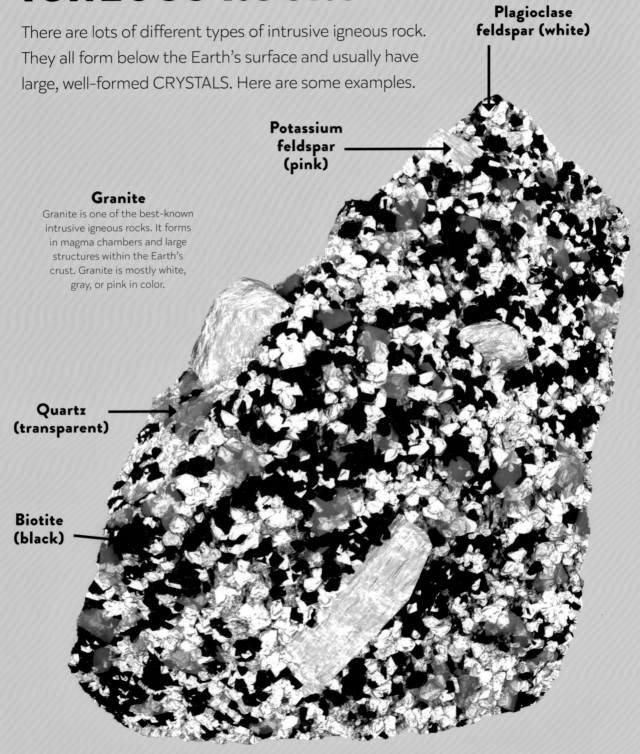

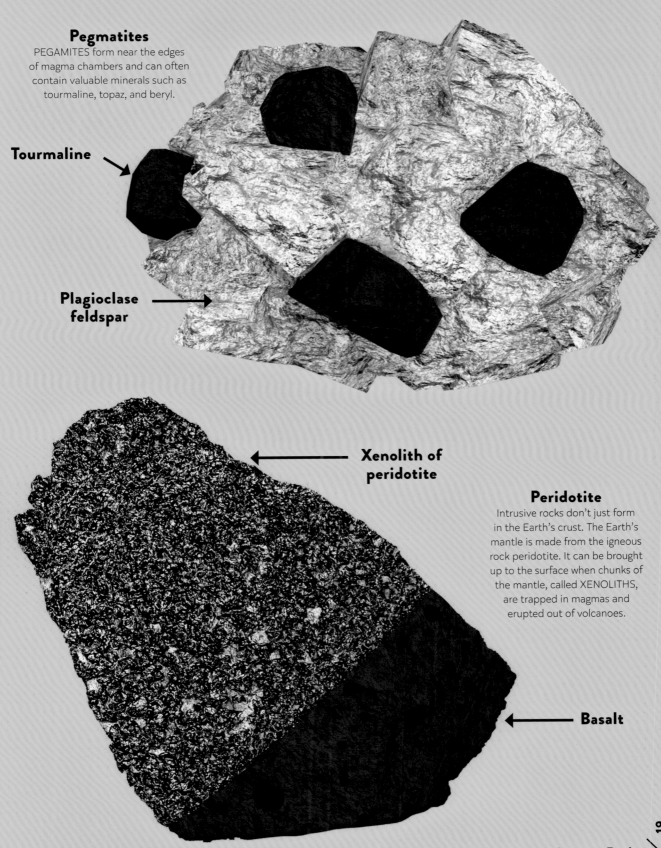

Pegmatites

PEGAMITES form near the edges of magma chambers and can often contain valuable minerals such as tourmaline, topaz, and beryl.

Tourmaline

Plagioclase feldspar

Xenolith of peridotite

Peridotite

Intrusive rocks don't just form in the Earth's crust. The Earth's mantle is made from the igneous rock peridotite. It can be brought up to the surface when chunks of the mantle, called XENOLITHS, are trapped in magmas and erupted out of volcanoes.

Basalt

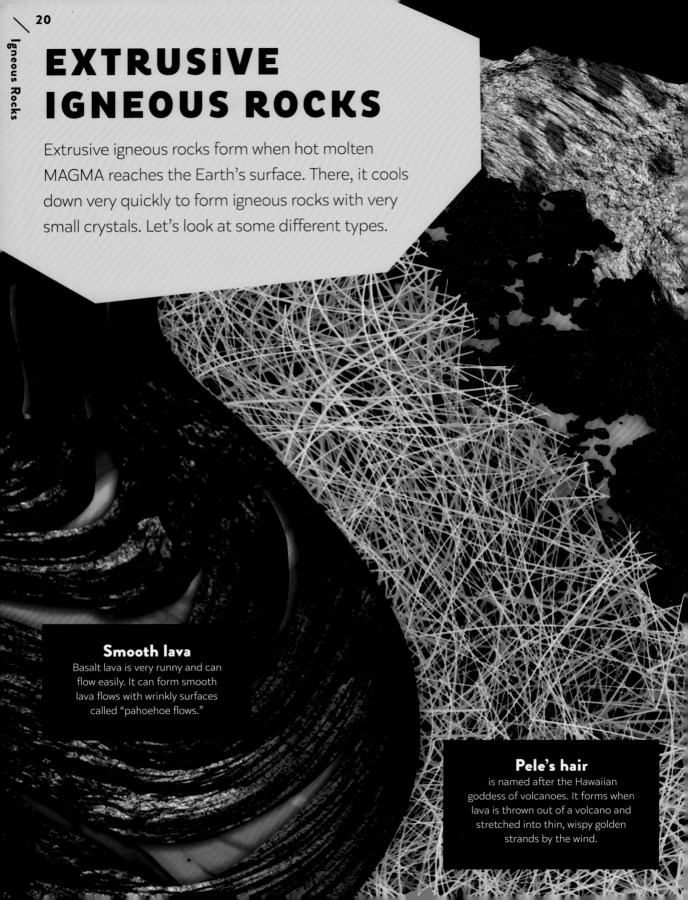

EXTRUSIVE IGNEOUS ROCKS

Extrusive igneous rocks form when hot molten MAGMA reaches the Earth's surface. There, it cools down very quickly to form igneous rocks with very small crystals. Let's look at some different types.

Smooth lava
Basalt lava is very runny and can flow easily. It can form smooth lava flows with wrinkly surfaces called "pahoehoe flows."

Pele's hair
is named after the Hawaiian goddess of volcanoes. It forms when lava is thrown out of a volcano and stretched into thin, wispy golden strands by the wind.

Obsidian
is a volcanic rock that is usually dark in color. It cools down so quickly there's no time for it to form any mineral crystals.

Pumice
is a pale-colored rock formed from frothy, gassy lava. Pumice solidifies very quickly and traps lots of gas bubbles. Because of all of this gas, pumice is really light and can float on water!

Blocky lava
If lava contains more silica, it means that the lava is thicker and more viscous. It tends to form, chunky, rubbly flows called "blocky lava." Andesite and rhyolite are common extrusive rocks that form blocky lava flows.

Feldspar

There are two important types of feldspars in igneous rocks, plagioclase and potassium FELDSPAR. They are very common minerals.

Plagioclase feldspar

Potassium feldspar

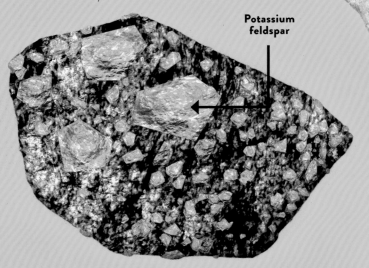

DID YOU KNOW?

The largest potassium feldspar crystal was found in Russia: it measured over 30 feet long! That's about the length of a bus.

IGNEOUS MINERALS

Igneous rocks are mostly made up of a group of minerals called SILICATES, which are formed from the element SILICON. Igneous minerals form during the cooling and solidification of molten rock. Which minerals solidify from molten rock all depends on three things: the chemistry of the magma, the temperature of the melt, and how quickly the magma is cooled down. In this section, we'll be looking at eight minerals that are commonly found in igneous rocks.

Quartz

Quartz is one of the most common minerals found at the Earth's surface! It is usually colorless and see-through, but a variety of colored quartz can occur in certain conditions. Although it forms in igneous rocks, quartz is also a very important mineral in metamorphic and sedimentary rocks.

Micas

Micas are a very common mineral in igneous rocks. They are different from other igneous minerals because they are very shiny and form in paper-thin, see-through sheets. There are two types, shown here.

Muscovite mica

Biotite mica

Pyroxene

Pyroxene is common in the basalt rocks found in volcanic areas like Hawaii.

Olivine

Olivine is easily recognizable for its rich green color. Olivine is common in basalt volcanic rocks found in Iceland, the Galapagos, and Hawaii. It is also one of the main minerals found in the Earth's mantle.

Hornblende, a type of amphibole

Amphibole

Amphibole is the name for a group of very dark-colored minerals found in igneous and metamorphic rocks.

WORLD WONDERS

Igneous rocks and formations have created some of the most spectacular landscapes in the world! In this section, we're going to investigate some of the most breathtaking ones.

KĪLAUEA LAVA FLOWS, HAWAII

The islands of Hawaii have some of the most spectacular volcanoes and lava flows anywhere in the world. Kīlauea has been erupting on-and-off for at least 2,800 years and nonstop since 1983! Kīlauea is just one of five volcanoes on the main island of Hawaii.

Kīlauea is famous for the special patterns that the lava forms as it flows away from the volcano. There are two well-known types, both of which are Hawaiian words. 'A'ā lava (pronounced "ah-ah") is a thick type of lava that has a rubbly and blocky surface, with blocks of cooling lava forming the outer layer. When cooled, this lava can be very hard to walk on because of all the loose, sharp material. Pāhoehoe (pronounced "pa-ho-ee-ho-ee") lava has a smooth surface that can sometimes form spectacular shapes that look like ripples or a pile of ropes – this is why it's sometimes called "ropy lava." Pāhoehoe lava tends to be quite thin and flows easily out of the volcano.

Pāhoehoe lava

ʻAʻā lava

DID YOU KNOW?
There are around 40,000 interlocking columns in the Giant's Causeway.

GIANT'S CAUSEWAY, NORTHERN IRELAND

The magnificent Giant's Causeway in Northern Ireland is made up of basalt forming what looks like a ripple of hexagons unfolding across the beach. This formation was created when huge lava flows erupted in the area. As this lava began to cool down and solidify, hexagonal fractures formed in the rock. This fracturing created the thousands of hexagon-shaped stepping stones you can see at the Giant's Causeway.

MOUNT EREBUS, ANTARCTICA

Mount Erebus is the most active volcano in Antarctica and is the most southerly volcano in the world! Erebus is constantly gurgling and spewing out gas and volcanic bombs. Its location in an icy environment means it has some unusual features. There are lots of ice caves on Erebus, which form when the hot gas coming from the volcano melts the surrounding ice. Some of the caves are topped with ice towers, which form when the steam coming out of the melting cave turns to ice in the freezing cold air. This creates strange frozen stacks across the icy landscape.

DID YOU KNOW?
The ice towers are caused by escaping steam. Some are almost 65 feet tall!

WHAT ARE SEDIMENTARY ROCKS?

Sedimentary rocks are the second type of rock in the rock cycle. They are the most common rocks on the Earth's surface, covering 75% of the land and over 90% of the sea floor! There are three main types of sedimentary rock: CLASTIC, chemical, and ORGANIC.

Clastic sedimentary rocks such as sandstone and mudstone are formed from tiny broken-up bits of other rocks that get squeezed and stuck together. Organic sedimentary rocks like coal and limestone are formed from the remains of ancient plants and animals. Chemical sedimentary rocks such as gypsum and halite are formed from the chemical processes of evaporation and precipitation. Let's take a closer look!

DID YOU KNOW?

Sedimentary rocks form in layers, called STRATA. Unless they have been tilted or folded, you will usually find older sedimentary strata at the bottom of a cliff, and younger strata at the top.

CLASTIC SEDIMENTARY ROCKS

Clastic sedimentary rocks are formed from fragments of other rocks that have been compacted and stuck together.

1. Over thousands of years, even the hardest rocks can get worn down. Frost, ice, running water, crashing waves, gases in the Earth's atmosphere, and even plant roots and burrowing animals can all break rocks down into smaller pieces, called "sediment."

2. Once it has been created, sediment is carried away by natural forces such as rivers, floods, glaciers, and winds. Sediment can be transported thousands of miles from where it started.

3. When a river reaches the sea or a glacier melts, it loses energy and dumps the sediment it is carrying. Layers of sediment settle at the bottom of lakes, oceans, riverbeds, and in desert sand dunes. These layers build up over time and start to squash the older sediments at the bottom. This squashing PRESSURE squeezes any water out of the sediments, like squeezing water from a sponge, and glues them together to form a CLASTIC SEDIMENTARY ROCK.

There are many different types of clastic sedimentary rock, here are some examples:

Sandstone
Sandstone is a clastic rock made up from millions of grains of sand.

Mudstone
Mudstone is a dark-colored rock formed from microscopic specks of mud and clay.

Conglomerate
These are rocks that are formed from a mixture of large rounded pebbles.

Breccia
Breccias are formed from large, jagged, smashed bits of rock.

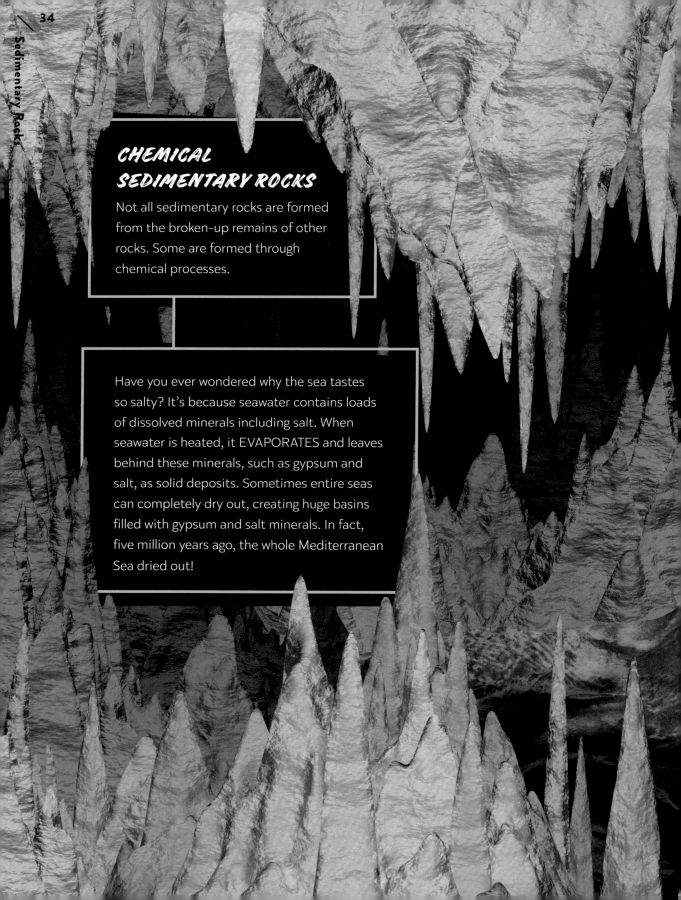

CHEMICAL SEDIMENTARY ROCKS

Not all sedimentary rocks are formed from the broken-up remains of other rocks. Some are formed through chemical processes.

Have you ever wondered why the sea tastes so salty? It's because seawater contains loads of dissolved minerals including salt. When seawater is heated, it EVAPORATES and leaves behind these minerals, such as gypsum and salt, as solid deposits. Sometimes entire seas can completely dry out, creating huge basins filled with gypsum and salt minerals. In fact, five million years ago, the whole Mediterranean Sea dried out!

Fresh water from lakes and rivers also contains dissolved minerals, including calcite, which is often left behind when water evaporates in caves. Over thousands of years, layers and layers of calcite build up into stalactites and stalagmites— structures that look like stone icicles!

Chemical limestone

CHEMICAL ROCK EXAMPLES

Gypsum

Halite

Sedimentary Rocks

ORGANIC SEDIMENTARY ROCKS

Some sedimentary rocks are formed from animal and plant material that gets cemented together. These rocks, called ORGANIC sedimentary rocks, often contain things like corals, shells, bones, leaves, roots, and microscopic marine creatures called PLANKTON. Organic sedimentary rocks form in a very similar way to clastic sedimentary rocks. Dead plant and animal material falls to the bottom of a sea, or lake, and piles up into thick layers. Over millions of years, these layers become buried, squashed, and cemented together to form organic sedimentary rocks like limestone, chalk, and coal.

Limestone

Limestone is a very common sedimentary rock formed from the mineral calcite. Limestone can be an organic sedimentary rock, made from marine plankton, corals, and seashells. It can also form as a chemical sedimentary rock.

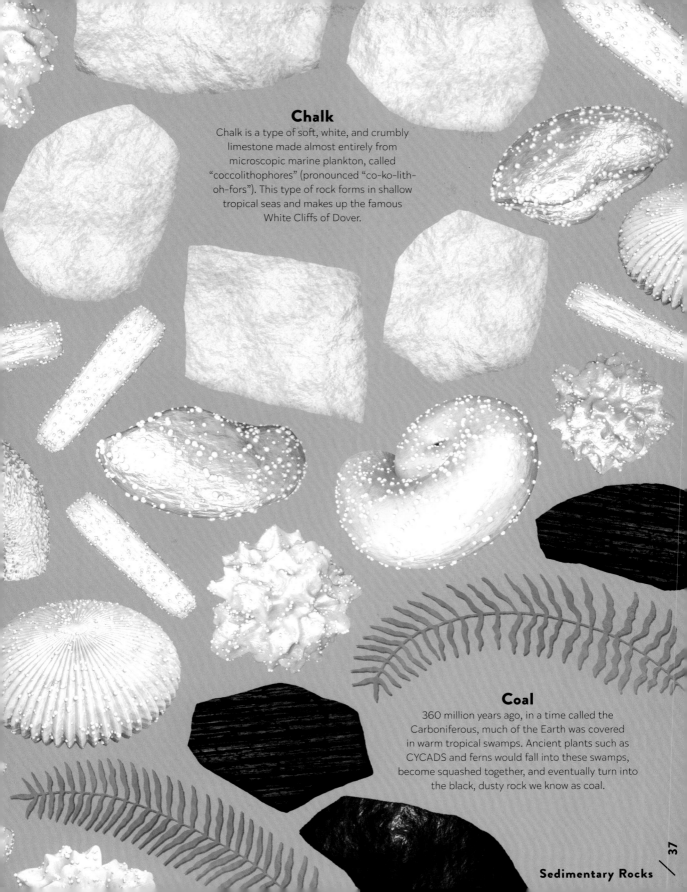

Chalk

Chalk is a type of soft, white, and crumbly limestone made almost entirely from microscopic marine plankton, called "coccolithophores" (pronounced "co-ko-lith-oh-fors"). This type of rock forms in shallow tropical seas and makes up the famous White Cliffs of Dover.

Coal

360 million years ago, in a time called the Carboniferous, much of the Earth was covered in warm tropical swamps. Ancient plants such as CYCADS and ferns would fall into these swamps, become squashed together, and eventually turn into the black, dusty rock we know as coal.

IDENTIFYING SEDIMENTARY ROCKS

Sedimentary minerals are divided into two main groups, depending on how the sedimentary rock was formed. There are sedimentary rocks that are made of broken-down bits of other rocks (these are called clastic sedimentary rocks). And then there are the rocks made up new minerals that form through chemical processes.

MINERALS IN CLASTIC SEDIMENTARY ROCKS

Many of the minerals found in these rocks you'll have seen before. These include common minerals such as quartz, feldspar, and mica (as we saw on page 22). The most important thing when sorting your clastic sedimentary rocks is to identify the shape and size of the grains in the rock. Grains can be everything from very jagged or "angular," like a piece of broken glass, to rounded and smooth like a beach pebble.

Rocks with very angular grains have not traveled very far before being deposited into a new rock—because none of the sharp edges have been knocked off. Rocks with smooth, rounded grains mean that the material was transported a long way, and the rough edges were eroded and worn down by water, ice, and wind before it was deposited in a new rock.

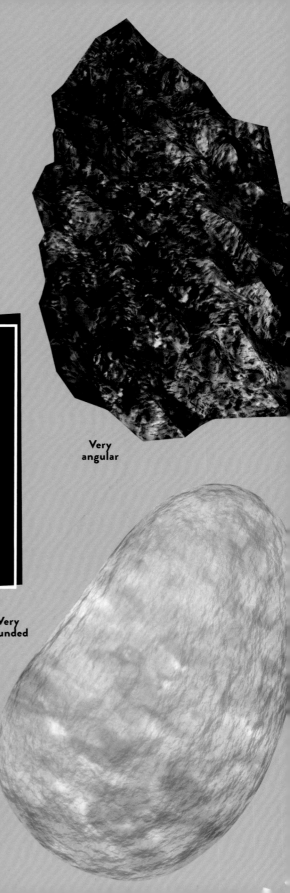

Very angular

Very rounded

MINERALS IN CHEMICAL SEDIMENTARY ROCKS

Chemical sedimentary rocks contain minerals that form from chemical processes such as evaporation or precipitation.

Gypsum

Gypsum is a white or see-through mineral, which forms when large areas of sea water evaporate—sometimes over millions of years. It can form as crystals or as layers.

Halite

Halite forms in the same way as gypsum but contains slightly different chemicals. Halite is also known by its more common name, "rock salt." This is the same salt that you shake onto your fries!

But it isn't just salt that is dissolved in sea water and fresh water. The various chemicals dissolved in the water can precipitate and fall to the bottom of the water and create new sedimentary rocks!

Calcite

One of the most important sedimentary minerals is calcite. Calcite is usually white and is one of the most common minerals at the surface of the Earth. It is the main mineral found in limestone, a very common rock, and it's also in chalk.

WORLD WONDERS

Sedimentary rocks and formations have also created some of the most spectacular landscapes in the world! Let's take a trip to three of the most interesting, although there are plenty more for you to discover in real life.

THE WAVE, ARIZONA, USA

"The Wave" rock is a mind-boggling red sandstone formation in the desert of Arizona in the USA. Famous for its unusual striped and wavy appearance, visitors come from all over the world to see it. The rocks show a series of desert dunes that have hardened and become frozen in time. The changes in direction of stripes, or layers, are caused by changes in the direction that the wind was blowing when the dunes were forming. The rocks are a window back in time into the desert conditions that existed here 200 million years ago, way back in the Jurassic period.

DID YOU KNOW?
Dinosaur footprints and even some dinosaur bones have been found in the sandstones of this area!

Sedimentary Rocks

HALONG BAY, VIETNAM

Halong Bay in north Vietnam is a beautiful tropical bay covered with large lumps of limestone rising up and towering over the rich blue waters. This type of formation is called KARST. Karst limestone occurs because of what happens when rainwater falls on limestone. Rainwater is slightly acidic (though not quite as acidic as something like lemon juice). When rainwater lands on limestone, it can dissolve the calcite in the rock and carry it away. Over time, this causes enormous amounts of erosion to happen, which can create unusual shapes and features, like those we see at Halong Bay. This process can also create interesting caves in the limestone.

DID YOU KNOW?
There are nearly 2,000 separate needle-like islands in Halong Bay!

Sedimentary Rocks

DID YOU KNOW?

The temperature and humidity in the cave is so high that scientists have to wear special cooling suits to enter the cave. They are not allow to stay inside for more than 45 minutes.

CAVE OF THE CRYSTALS, MEXICO

This cave in Mexico contains some of the largest gypsum crystals ever found, the largest being 40 feet long. That's taller than two giraffes standing on top of each other! The temperatures in these caves can reach 136°F. The unusual environment of very high temperatures in a cave sealed off from the outside world has led to the growth of these enormous crystals.

WHAT IS A FOSSIL?

FOSSILS are the remains and traces of prehistoric plants and animals preserved in sedimentary rocks. Finding and studying fossils can tell us about the extraordinary creatures that once roamed the ancient continents and swam through the primeval seas.

There are two main types of fossils: body fossils and trace fossils. Body fossils are the most common fossils found on Earth. They are formed from the remains of animals and plants—things like bones, teeth, leaves, branches, and shells. Trace fossils are signs left behind by ancient animal and plant life. They can be footprints, nests, imprints of leaves or shells, burrows, and even fossilized poop!

DID
YOU KNOW?
Some of the oldest animal fossils on Earth
come from the rocks of the Burgess Shale in
Canada. These fossils provide a remarkable
snapshot of life 500 million years ago, when
creatures like the predatory *Anomalocaris*,
the spiny *Hallucigenia,* and the five-eyed
Opabinia would have lived in the
ancient seas.

HOW DO FOSSILS FORM?

Most fossils form when living things are turned into stone. For this to happen, an animal or plant must be buried soon after it has died, before it rots away or is eaten by scavenging animals. Let's take an ichthyosaur, a Jurassic marine reptile, to see how a fossil might form:

Tar and amber

Fossils can form when animals and plants get caught up in sticky materials like TAR and tree resin. These materials harden over time and can preserve trapped plants and animals in amazing detail. Lots of the fossils we have from the most recent ice age were preserved in tar pits.

An ichthyosaur dies and falls to the bottom of the sea, where it becomes buried in mud.

Over time, layers of mud and sand build up on top of the ichthyosaur and it becomes squashed. The fleshy parts of the ichthyosaur decay away, but minerals dissolved in underground water seep into the ichthyosaur's bones and turn them into stone. This process is called fossilization and it usually takes millions of years.

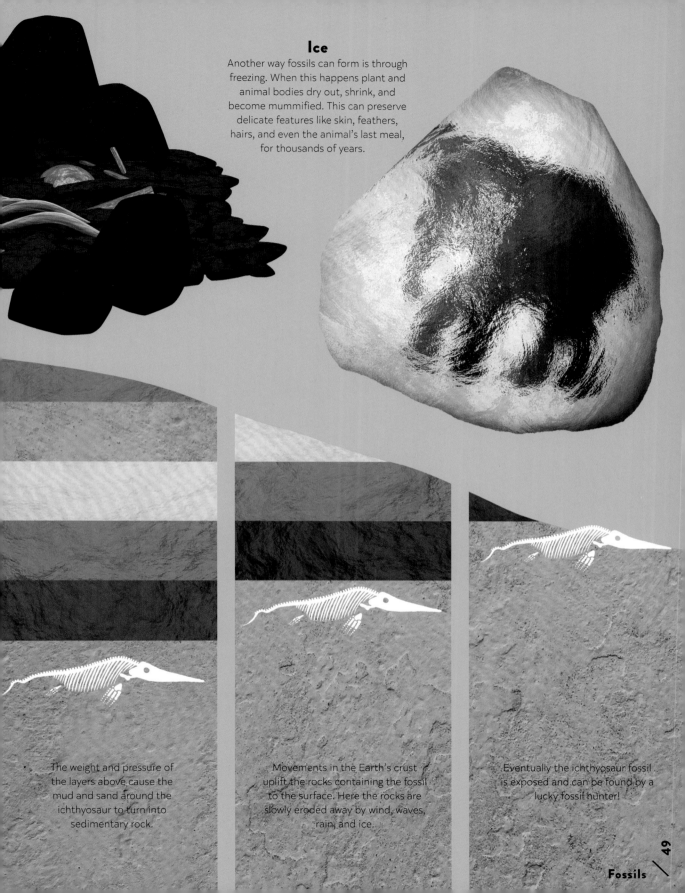

Ice

Another way fossils can form is through freezing. When this happens plant and animal bodies dry out, shrink, and become mummified. This can preserve delicate features like skin, feathers, hairs, and even the animal's last meal, for thousands of years.

The weight and pressure of the layers above cause the mud and sand around the ichthyosaur to turn into sedimentary rock.

Movements in the Earth's crust uplift the rocks containing the fossil to the surface. Here the rocks are slowly eroded away by wind, waves, rain, and ice.

Eventually the ichthyosaur fossil is exposed and can be found by a lucky fossil hunter!

Corals

You might not realize it, but corals are actually animals. They evolved over 500 million years ago, in the Cambrian period, and have been living in our warm shallow seas ever since.

Ammonites

Probably the most well-known invertebrate fossils, ammonites lived in the Jurassic period and were similar to modern-day squid. They propelled themselves through the sea by squirting jets of water from inside their spiral shells.

INVERTEBRATE FOSSILS

Like modern animals, fossil animals are divided up into VERTEBRATES and INVERTEBRATES—animals with backbones and animals without backbones. Invertebrate fossils are the most common fossils that are found.

Trilobites

Trilobites are related to modern-day scorpions and crustaceans. They had large eyes made from thousands of tiny lenses and armored skeletons that they shed as they grew. Trilobites lived in the seas for more than 250 million years, before becoming extinct at the end of Permian period.

Crinoids

These bizarre animals lived in large colonies attached to rocks on the seabed or to floating pieces of driftwood. They evolved 500 million years ago, and there are still a few species around today.

Bivalves

Bivalves are shelled animals like oysters, scallops, and mussels. *Gryphaea*, also known as "devil's toenail" because of its shape, is a very common bivalve found in Jurassic limestone rocks.

VERTEBRATE FOSSILS

Vertebrate fossils are the fossilized remains of animals with backbones. There are thousands of different types of vertebrate fossils, from tiny shrews up to gigantic dinosaurs. Here are some famous examples:

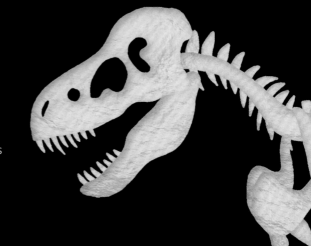

Archaeopteryx

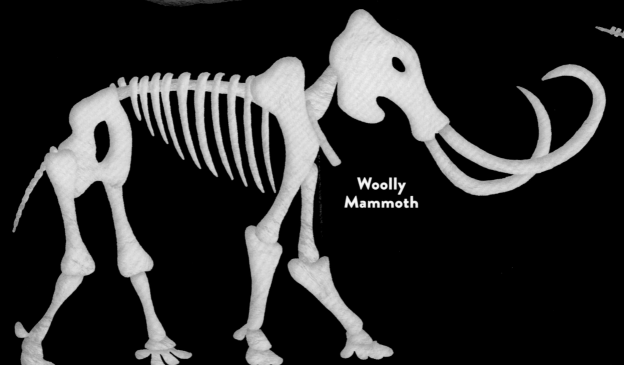

Woolly Mammoth

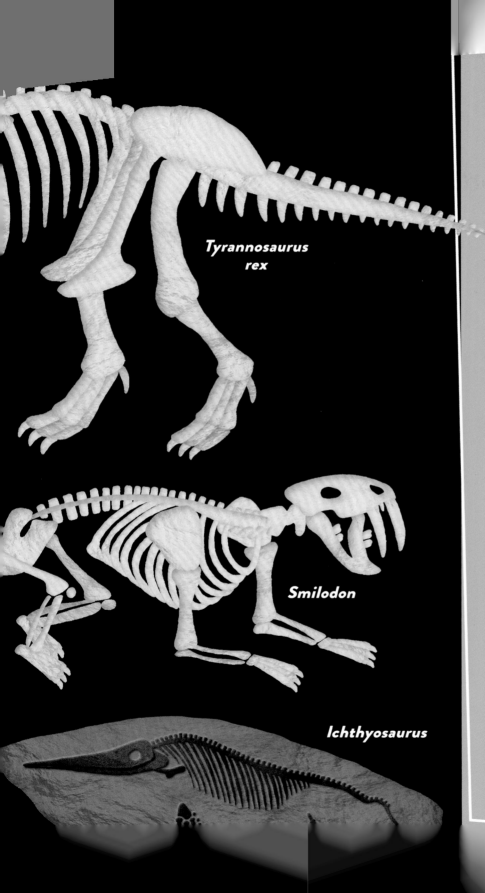

Tyrannosaurus rex

Smilodon

Ichthyosaurus

Archaeopteryx
Although it looks like a bird, *Archaeopteryx* is actually a Jurassic dinosaur. It had feathers and wings and may have been able to fly or glide between trees.

Tyrannosaurus rex
This fearsome dinosaur evolved in the Cretaceous period. It had huge, sharp teeth, and its jaws were so strong it could crush bone.

Smilodon
This saber-toothed cat lived in the last ice age. Its huge front teeth, or sabers, combined with its muscular front paws, are thought to have been used to puncture the necks of its prey.

Woolly Mammoth
One of the most famous fossils, the woolly mammoth, went extinct around 10,000 years ago. As their name suggests, they were covered in a thick layer of hair, essential for keeping them warm in the freezing temperatures of the last ice age.

Ichthyosaurus
This marine reptile looked a bit like a prehistoric dolphin. It had huge eyes and extremely sharp teeth for feasting on ammonites, fish, and even other ichthyosaurs.

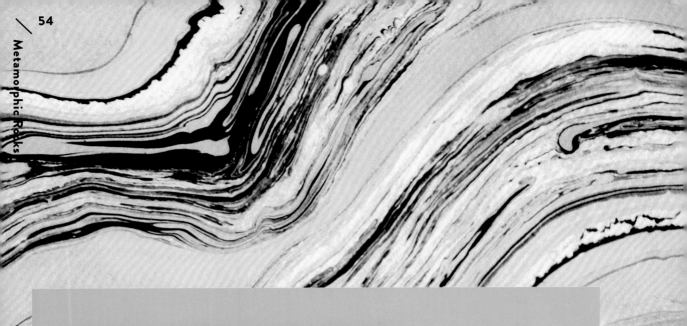

WHAT ARE METAMORPHIC ROCKS?

Metamorphic rocks are one of the three main rock types in the rock cycle, along with igneous and sedimentary. They are formed from the squashed and heated remains of igneous and sedimentary rocks.

Trying to squash or squeeze most rocks with your hands is very difficult because they are very hard and strong, but deep within the Earth, the pressures and temperatures are higher than you could imagine. Temperatures can get all the way up to 1,300°F in the crust—that's seven times hotter than boiling water! The weight of all those rocks sitting on top of them causes the rocks to behave almost like modeling clay: they can be twisted, heated, crumpled, and transformed into completely different rocks. This process is called METAMORPHISM.

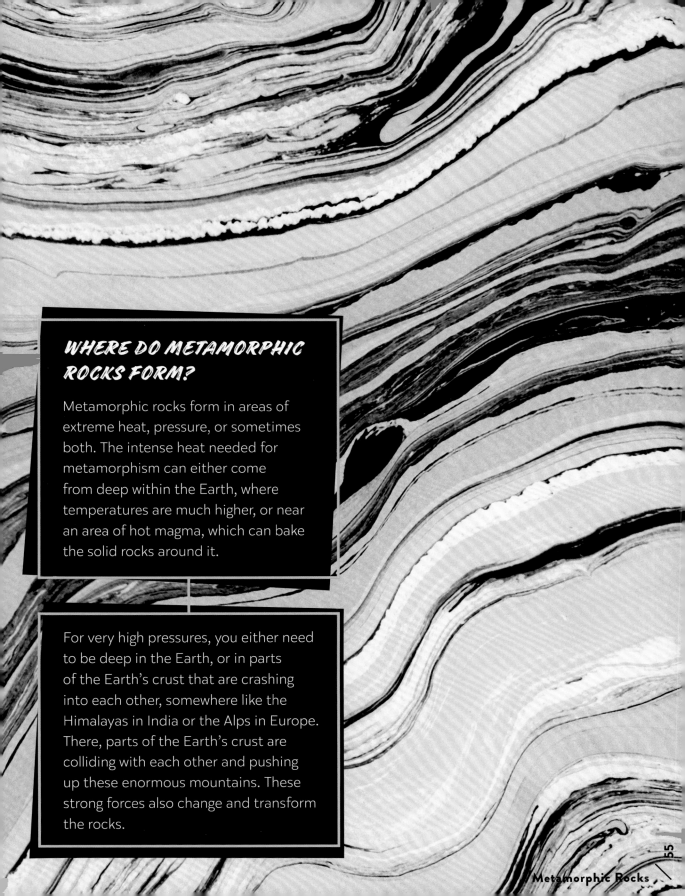

WHERE DO METAMORPHIC ROCKS FORM?

Metamorphic rocks form in areas of extreme heat, pressure, or sometimes both. The intense heat needed for metamorphism can either come from deep within the Earth, where temperatures are much higher, or near an area of hot magma, which can bake the solid rocks around it.

For very high pressures, you either need to be deep in the Earth, or in parts of the Earth's crust that are crashing into each other, somewhere like the Himalayas in India or the Alps in Europe. There, parts of the Earth's crust are colliding with each other and pushing up these enormous mountains. These strong forces also change and transform the rocks.

HOW DO THEY FORM?

There are three different ways that rocks can be affected by heat and pressure to form metamorphic rocks...

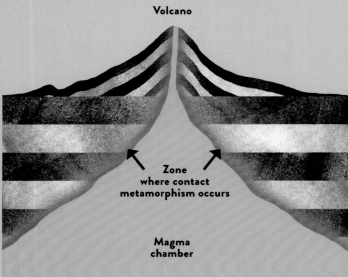

Volcano

Zone where contact metamorphism occurs

Magma chamber

Contact metamorphism

This is when heat from molten rock causes the surrounding rocks to transform. In this situation, the temperature change is more important than the pressure change.

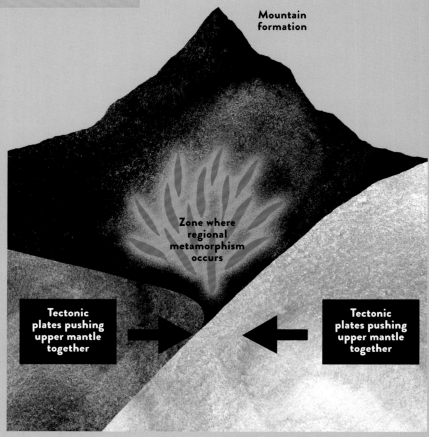

Mountain formation

Regional metamorphism

This is when rocks are buried deep in the crust, often over 6 miles deep, and where the temperature is hotter! The weight of the rocks above them, and the force of tectonic plates moving toward each other, can cause the rocks to transform. These rocks often form at the roots of big mountain ranges, like the Himalayas.

Deep within the Earth, the pressures are extremely high, but they are not the same in all directions. For example, when mountains are forming, the pressure is much higher in the direction shown.

Zone where regional metamorphism occurs

Tectonic plates pushing upper mantle together

Tectonic plates pushing upper mantle together

Hydrothermal metamorphism

There is a third type of metamorphism called "hydrothermal metamorphism". This is where hot fluids containing lots of chemicals, pass through the rock. As they move through the rocks they can change the minerals and also deposit new ones.

DID YOU KNOW?

Hydrothermal metamorphism is often responsible for important mineral deposits of gold and copper!

HOW DO THE ROCKS TRANSFORM?

The reason we see rocks at the surface of the Earth is because enormous forces within the crust push and squeeze these rocks up to the surface. They then become exposed by erosion and we can see them!

Heat and pressure can have a huge impact on rocks. Pressure can twist and squeeze them. Heat can rearrange the minerals in the rock to form new patterns. It can also cause minerals to break down and form a new set of minerals in the new metamorphic rock.

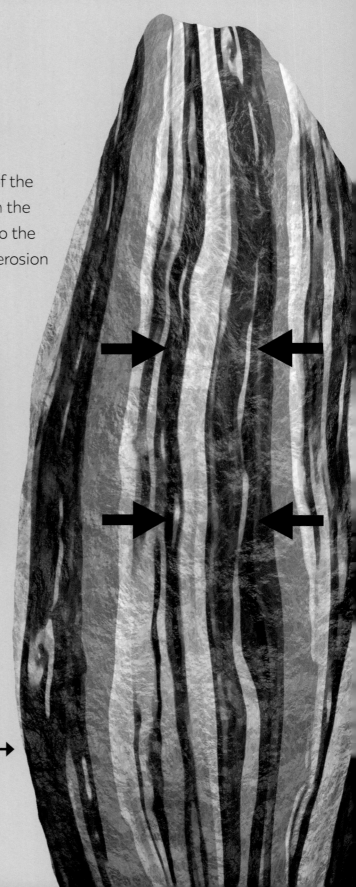

If a piece of rock is heated up and squashed very, very hard, then the flat-shaped minerals in the rock start to grow in bands. This creates lines in the rock, or "banding."

When the rock is squeezed in this direction, it causes the minerals to grow in the opposite direction. This makes bands form in this orientation.

We can see the bands in the rock because they are picked out by different colored minerals, giving the rock a striped look.

The amount of banding in the rock is linked to the "metamorphic grade." This means the more heat and pressure, the greater the change, the higher the metamorphic grade.

To explore this, we're going to take the journey of a rock passing through the different metamorphic grades and see what it looks like! We'll start with a mudstone that we find at the bottom of the sea—what happens next?

INCREASING METAMORPHISM

Slate

If we add a little bit of heat and pressure, the first metamorphic rock we form out of mudstone is a *slate*! You'll probably have seen slate quite a lot—it's useful for lots of things like roof tiles, floors, and pavements. You can often break a slate by hand to form long, flat sheets. You can't see it, but this is because the mica minerals have lined up in the rock, making it easier to break along these bands. This is a low-grade metamorphic rock.

Phyllite

If we add a bit more heat and pressure to the slate, we get a rock called *phyllite* (pronounced "fill-ite"). This is quite similar to slate, but is often shinier. That is because the shiny mica minerals have lined up even more to give a shiny appearance. Phyllite is usually gray or black.

Schist

If we add even more heat and pressure to the rock, we get a sparkly rock called *schist*. In schist, the shiny micas have grown so much that we can see individual crystals with our eyes. Banding starts to appear. This is a medium-grade metamorphic rock.

Gneiss

Then, at even higher pressures and at temperatures above around 900°F, we get to the high-grade rock, *gneiss* (pronounced "nice"). Gneiss often has black and white stripes. These are caused by the layers of light minerals, such as quartz and feldspar and layers of dark minerals such as biotite mica and garnet that have formed bands during metamorphism.

As we've seen on the previous pages, the type of metamorphic rock you get depends very much on the amount of heat and pressure, and the rock you had to start with! Let's explore some different types here.

Hornfels (and spotted hornfels)

Hornfels is a very hard gray-black rock. It forms when molten rock forms near a mudstone. The heat then transforms the mudstone into a rock called hornfels.

DID YOU KNOW?

There is a special kind of hornfels that can form called "spotted hornfels." This happens when dark spots form on the rock where crystals of new minerals have started to grow. These are often minerals called cordierite or andalusite.

Quartzite

Quartzite is the rock that you end up with when you metamorphose sandstones containing quartz. The heat and pressure cause the sand grains, made up of quartz, to re-form and become stuck together by silica. This makes a very strong network of interlocking quartz grains, making this a very good rock to use in building.

Sand grains under the microscope **Interlocking quartz grains**

Marble

Marble is a very famous rock that has been used in sculpture and buildings for thousands of years. Marble is formed when the sedimentary rock limestone is metamorphosed. Similar to the quartz in quartzite, the calcite in the limestone re-forms to create interlocking crystals. Marble is softer than quartzite, so it is easy to carve and sculpt into statues, like the ancient Romans did!

Blueschist

Blueschist is named after its beautiful blue color. It is formed when basalt is metamorphosed at high pressures and lower temperatures. The blue comes from the growth of the minerals glaucophane and lawsonite during metamorphism.

Eclogite

Eclogite is a very pretty green-and-red rock. Like blueschist, it forms when the igneous rock basalt is metamorphosed but forms at higher pressures and temperatures than blueschist. The red color comes from the large garnet crystals surrounded by small crystals of green pyroxene.

METAMORPHIC MINERALS

When a rock is metamorphosed, its minerals are heated and squeezed under extreme temperatures and pressures deep within the Earth's crust. The chemicals that once made up igneous and sedimentary minerals can be broken down and completely rearranged into brand-new metamorphic minerals.

Some minerals only appear in metamorphic rocks. These minerals are very useful because they form at different temperatures and pressures. This means that they can be used to figure out how much heat and pressure the rock has been under during its metamorphism. For example, the mineral most likely to form at a pressure of 2 kilobars and a temperature of 500°C (930°F) would be andalusite.

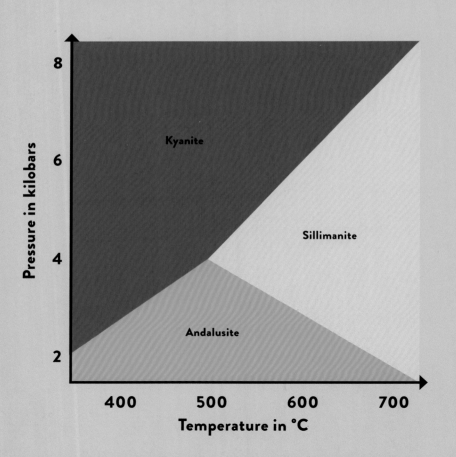

Andalusite, kyanite, and sillimanite are all made of the same chemicals. However, under different pressures and temperatures they have different CRYSTAL STRUCTURES.

Andalusite

Andalusite is a pink or gray mineral that forms when a rock is metamorphosed under low pressures. It is usually found in metamorphic rocks such as slate and hornfels.

Sillimanite

Sillimanite is a white mineral that usually forms microscopic crystals. It is found in schists and gneisses that have been under high pressures, but also under scorching temperatures of at least 930°F.

Kyanite

Bright blue kyanite forms long, bladed crystals. It forms under very high pressures in schists and gneisses.

Mercury

Venus

Earth

Mars

The Sun

Rock planets

ALL ABOUT SPACE ROCKS

Believe it or not, rocks form in space as well as on Earth. In fact, much of our Solar System is made from rock. From the inner rocky planets of Mercury, Venus, Mars, and Earth, to the small moons that orbit around each planet, and the asteroid belt between Mars and Jupiter, it is all made from rock!

MARS ROCKS

Mars is mostly made from the igneous rock basalt, like our moon. Its coloring comes from the metal iron, which rusts to a red color in the thin Martian atmosphere. Unlike our moon, Mars also has sedimentary rocks on its surface. Sandstones on Mars indicate that it once had large sandy desert dunes. Conglomerates, formed from rounded pebbles, tell us that Mars once had flowing rivers—and mudstones show that it also used to have large lakes of water.

Neil Armstrong's footprint in the LUNAR REGOLITH

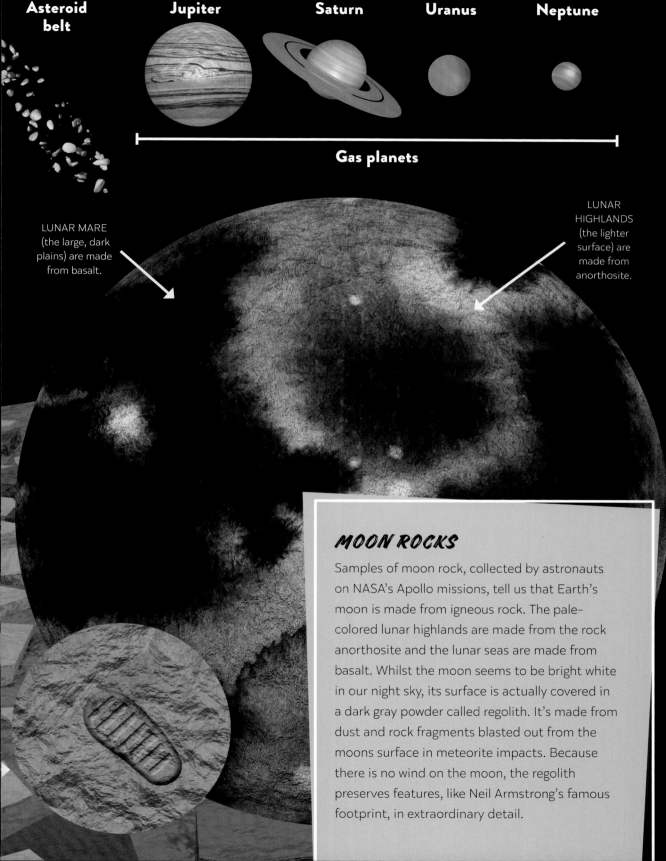

Asteroid belt

Jupiter

Saturn

Uranus

Neptune

Gas planets

LUNAR MARE (the large, dark plains) are made from basalt.

LUNAR HIGHLANDS (the lighter surface) are made from anorthosite.

MOON ROCKS

Samples of moon rock, collected by astronauts on NASA's Apollo missions, tell us that Earth's moon is made from igneous rock. The pale-colored lunar highlands are made from the rock anorthosite and the lunar seas are made from basalt. Whilst the moon seems to be bright white in our night sky, its surface is actually covered in a dark gray powder called regolith. It's made from dust and rock fragments blasted out from the moons surface in meteorite impacts. Because there is no wind on the moon, the regolith preserves features, like Neil Armstrong's famous footprint, in extraordinary detail.

METEORITES

Meteorites are mixtures of rock and metal that fall from space to the Earth's surface.

Almost all of the meteorites we get on Earth come from the asteroid belt, a junkyard of rock and metal between Mars and Jupiter that never managed to form a planet. The asteroid belt is very crowded, so sometimes asteroids collide with each other and get knocked off course. Occasionally, the paths of these asteroids can overlap with the Earth's orbit and get pulled in by the Earth's gravity.

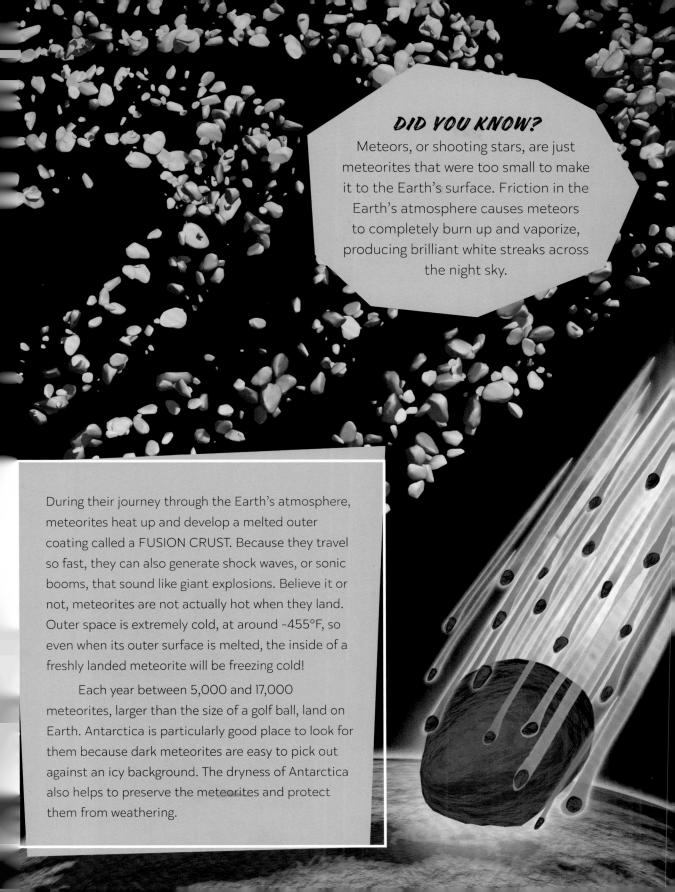

During their journey through the Earth's atmosphere, meteorites heat up and develop a melted outer coating called a FUSION CRUST. Because they travel so fast, they can also generate shock waves, or sonic booms, that sound like giant explosions. Believe it or not, meteorites are not actually hot when they land. Outer space is extremely cold, at around -455°F, so even when its outer surface is melted, the inside of a freshly landed meteorite will be freezing cold!

Each year between 5,000 and 17,000 meteorites, larger than the size of a golf ball, land on Earth. Antarctica is particularly good place to look for them because dark meteorites are easy to pick out against an icy background. The dryness of Antarctica also helps to preserve the meteorites and protect them from weathering.

Meteorites formed at the same time as the early Solar System, around 4,570 million years ago. Studying them can help geologists understand how the planets in the Solar System formed. There are four main types of meteorite: stony meteorites, iron meteorites, stony-iron meteorites, and achondrites.

Stony meteorites

Stony meteorites, also known as chondrites, have never been completely melted. They are made from a jumbled mixture of minerals, similar to those in the Earth's crust and mantle, as well as flecks of iron and nickel metal.

Iron meteorites

If a chondrite meteorite is heated to between 1,800 and 2,400°F, it will start to melt. First, the iron and nickel melt to form metal blobs, which sink toward the center of the asteroid and create a metal core. Iron meteorites come from the metal cores of these melted asteroids. When they are sliced open, iron meteorites can display a unique criss-cross pattern, known as a "Widmanstätten pattern."

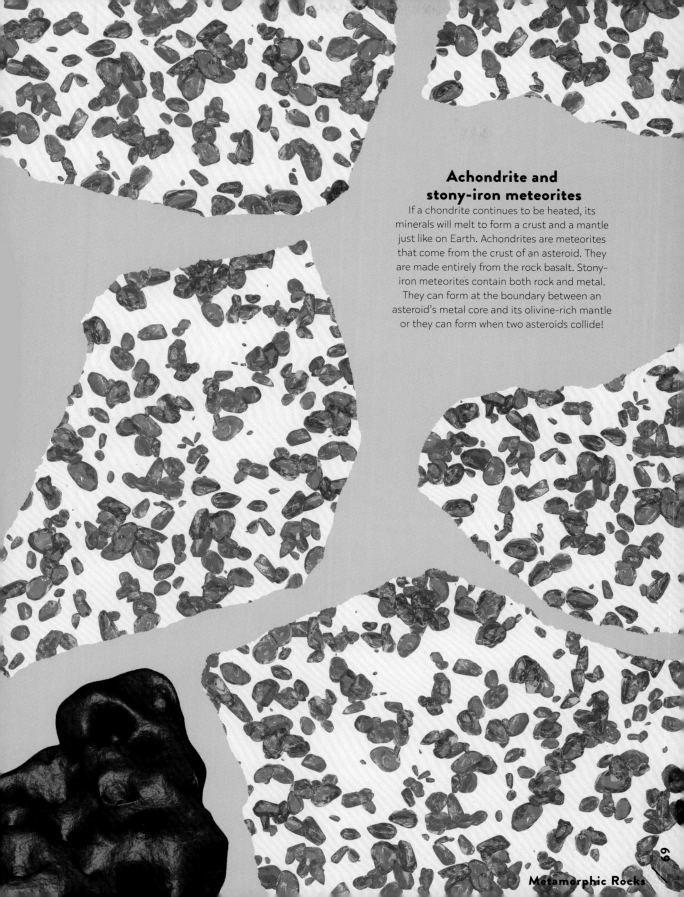

Achondrite and stony-iron meteorites

If a chondrite continues to be heated, its minerals will melt to form a crust and a mantle just like on Earth. Achondrites are meteorites that come from the crust of an asteroid. They are made entirely from the rock basalt. Stony-iron meteorites contain both rock and metal. They can form at the boundary between an asteroid's metal core and its olivine-rich mantle or they can form when two asteroids collide!

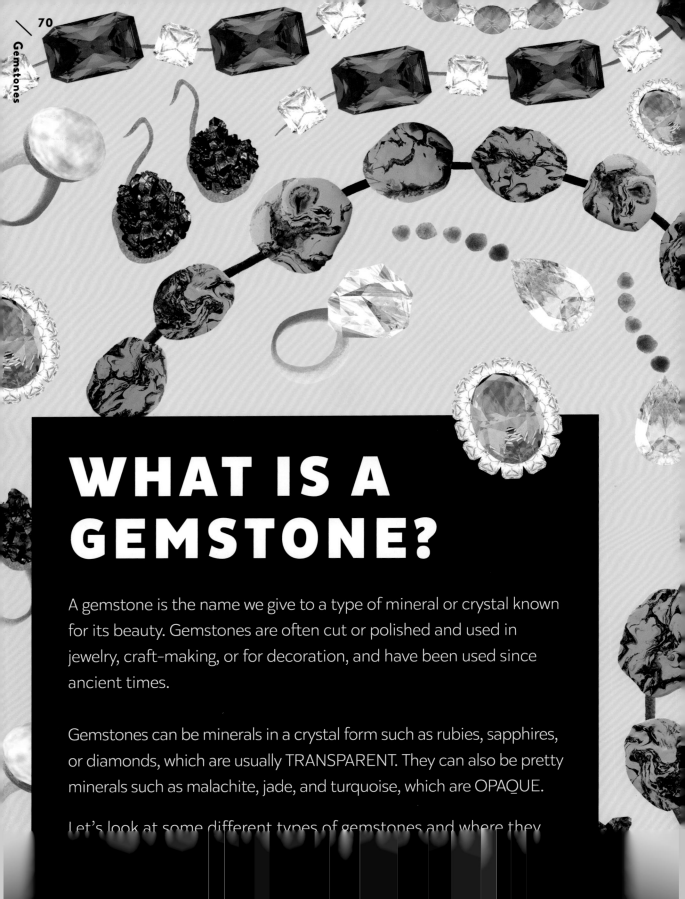

WHAT IS A GEMSTONE?

A gemstone is the name we give to a type of mineral or crystal known for its beauty. Gemstones are often cut or polished and used in jewelry, craft-making, or for decoration, and have been used since ancient times.

Gemstones can be minerals in a crystal form such as rubies, sapphires, or diamonds, which are usually TRANSPARENT. They can also be pretty minerals such as malachite, jade, and turquoise, which are OPAQUE.

Let's look at some different types of gemstones and where they

LAPIS LAZULI is a beautiful, intense blue gemstone that has been used for thousands of years because of its beauty. It was used by the ancient Egyptians to make pieces of jewelry and it was even used in Pharaoh Tutankhamun's dazzling funeral mask. The Egyptian ruler Cleopatra used lapis lazuli as eyeshadow!

DID YOU KNOW?

Although diamond is considered to be the queen of gemstones, there are many gemstones that are rarer than diamonds. Two of the rarest gemstones are tanzanite and alexandrite, both of which show beautiful shifts in color depending on lighting. Jadeite, a form of jade, is also very rare. In 1997, a jadeite necklace was sold for nearly 10 million dollars!

DID YOU KNOW?

The Taj Mahal in India is decorated with different kinds of precious and semiprecious gemstones. These include jade, turquoise, lapis lazuli, rubies, and jasper.

GEODES

Sometimes conditions are just right for crystals to grow in a very special way that creates large dazzling deposits called GEODES

On the outside, they may look like a totally plain rock, but on the inside they have a secret...they are full of spectacular and beautiful mineral deposits

Geodes can form from many different gemstones. One of the most common minerals is amethyst, which can create wonderful purple formations. Other minerals include agate, pyrite, and opal

Amethyst

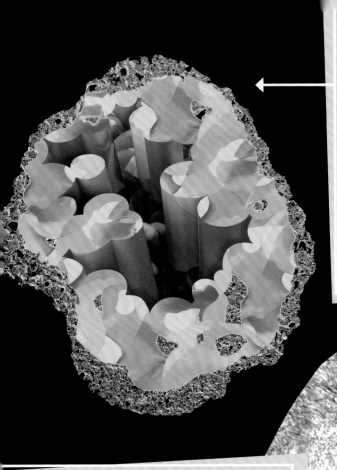

SEDIMENTARY GEODES

Sedimentary geodes form in gaps and holes in sedimentary rock such as limestone. They are usually smaller than volcanic geodes and sometimes form in the holes that are left behind when the soft parts of animals and plants decay and leave behind a space for them to grow in. This can even result in spectacular geodes forming in shells and corals.

VOLCANIC GEODES

Sometimes when volcanic rocks cool, holes and gaps form as part of the rock. This is because gas bubbles get trapped in the molten rock. Over time, water passes through the rock. This water can be hot or cold and often carries minerals dissolved in the water. As the water moves through the rock, it leaves behind small amounts of minerals that build up over time, producing geodes. Volcanic geodes are the most popular and are often the biggest.

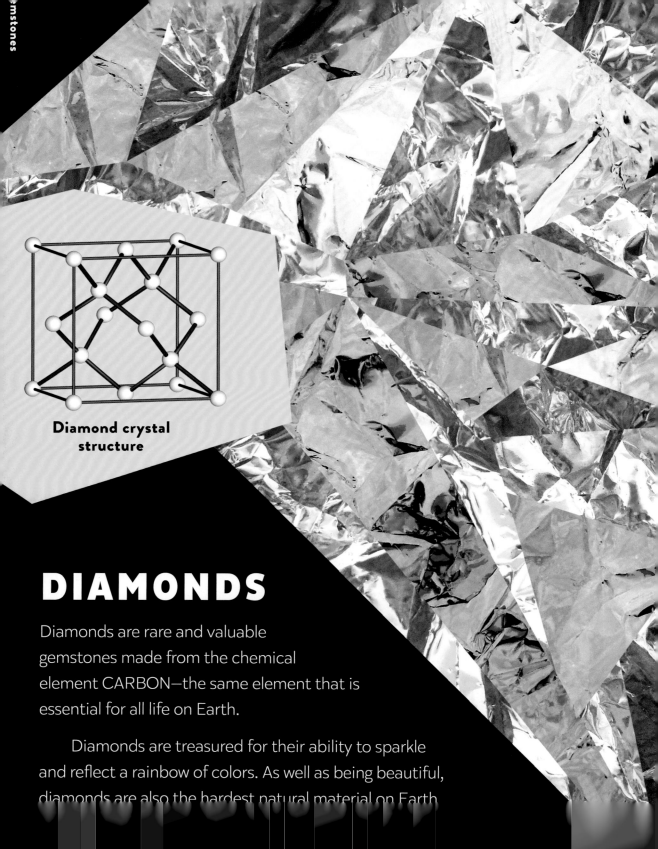

**Diamond crystal
structure**

DIAMONDS

Diamonds are rare and valuable
gemstones made from the chemical
element CARBON—the same element that is
essential for all life on Earth.

Diamonds are treasured for their ability to sparkle
and reflect a rainbow of colors. As well as being beautiful,
diamonds are also the hardest natural material on Earth

HOW ARE THEY FORMED?

Diamonds begin life hundreds of miles beneath our feet in the Earth's mantle. Here they form under crushing pressures and scorching temperatures of more than 1,800°F! Diamonds can be discovered on the surface when they are brought up in rare volcanic rocks, called KIMBERLITES. Initially kimberlites start out as pockets of magma deep within the mantle. When conditions are right, they can erupt violently toward the Earth's surface creating structures, called volcanic pipes.

As they rocket upward, kimberlite magmas rip up chunks of the upper mantle, including rocks that might contain diamonds, and transport them to the surface like a conveyor belt. Most kimberlites, and so most diamonds, are found in CRATONS, these are ancient areas of continental crust that are over one billion years old.

Kimberlite

Pipes carry diamonds up

Diamond formation zone

Magma chamber

SPOTTING GUIDE

When you think of a typical diamond, you probably imagine a clear, shimmering gemstone. However, in reality, diamonds are rarely this clear, and when the slightest shift occurs in a diamond's crystal structure, it becomes colorful.

Green

In the case of green diamonds, it is natural radiation in the rocks surrounding the diamond that can produce this color. This harmless radiation can blemish its surface and make it appear green.

Colorless

When there are no impurities or imperfections, diamonds are colorless.

Yellow and brown

If NITROGEN replaces some of a diamond's carbon atoms, it can take on a yellow or pale brown tint.

Red and pink

Red and pink diamonds are exceptionally rare. These beautiful colors can be produced when the structure of a diamond crystal is distorted during its rocky journey from the deep mantle up to the Earth's surface.

Blue

Blue diamonds can be produced when minuscule amounts of the chemical element BORON get into the crystal structure.

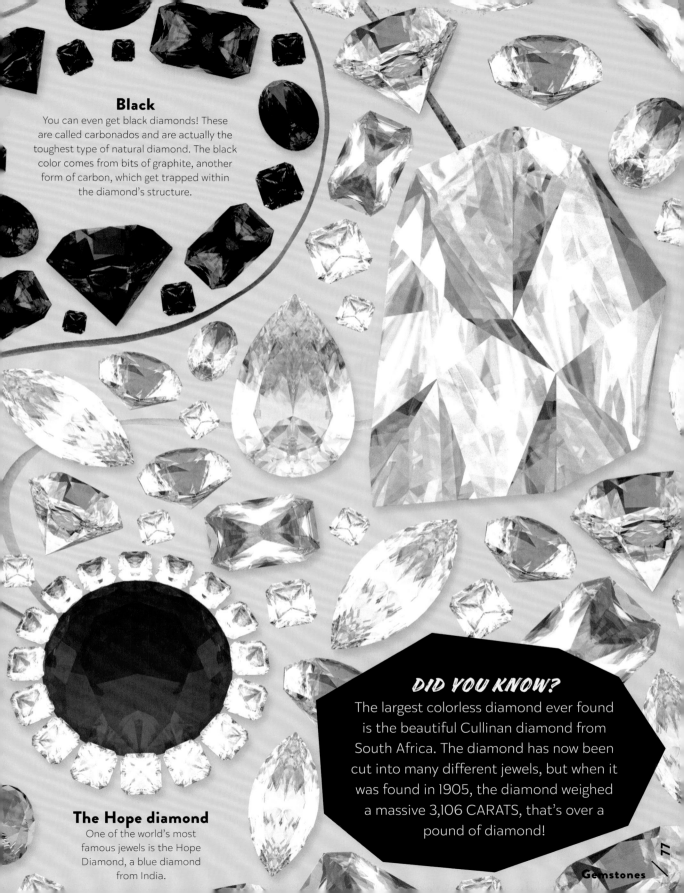

Black

You can even get black diamonds! These are called carbonados and are actually the toughest type of natural diamond. The black color comes from bits of graphite, another form of carbon, which get trapped within the diamond's structure.

The Hope diamond
One of the world's most famous jewels is the Hope Diamond, a blue diamond from India.

DID YOU KNOW?
The largest colorless diamond ever found is the beautiful Cullinan diamond from South Africa. The diamond has now been cut into many different jewels, but when it was found in 1905, the diamond weighed a massive 3,106 CARATS, that's over a pound of diamond!

OPALS

An opal is a colorful and shimmery gemstone used in beautiful jewelry and decorative designs. Nearly all of the world's opals are found in Australia or Ethiopia, and most of them are between 15 and 20 million years old! Opals have been fascinating people with their colors and beauty since as far back as the Roman times.

There are many different types of opal in lots of beautiful colors. The two main types of opals are "common opals" and "precious opals." Common opals are the least pretty ones: they come in duller colors and are often cloudy or milky-looking. It is precious opals that are used in making jewelry and ornament decoration.

Light opal

Boulder opal

HOW ARE THEY FORMED?

Opals are formed deep underground in cracks and holes in the rock. Opal is made up of a material called silica, which is found in sandstone. As water moves through sandstone, it dissolves the silica into the water and carries it away through the rock layers underground. Sometimes the water collects in cracks and spaces underground, and over time the water evaporates, leaving behind a silica deposit. A deposit is the material left behind when all of the water has gone, like when sea water evaporates and salt is left behind!

Opalized fossil

For opal to form, you need the silica material left behind to form in layers of silica arranged in tiny spheres. This process is extremely slow, and it can take millions of years for just half an inch of opal to form. Opal can form in any type of hole or crack found in the rock layers, and sometimes this happens in fossils in the gaps left behind after the animal has decayed.

Dark opal

Fire opal

CORUNDUM

Believe it or not, you've probably seen corundum before. Corundum is actually the scientific mineral name for the two popular gemstones: ruby and sapphire.

Corundum is almost as hard as diamond. It forms in igneous and metamorphic rocks. Like diamond, corundum is colorless when pure, however it commonly contains small amounts of other metals, which can produce a range of different colors. To be classed as a ruby, corundum must be a deep pinky-red color. This ruby color, sometimes more gruesomely known as "pigeon blood red," comes from the presence of CHROMIUM.

STAR SAPPHIRES AND RUBIES

Star sapphires and star rubies are rare types of corundum that display shimmering six-pointed stars of light just below their surfaces. These striking and beautiful features are known as ASTERISMS. The Star of Adam from Sri Lanka is the largest known star sapphire and weighs over 1,400 carats.

BERYL AND TOURMALINE

Aquamarine
is pale sky-blue
because of iron.

Morganite
This beautiful peachy,
rose-pink color comes
from MAGNESIUM atoms.

BERYL

The mineral beryl is probably best known for the beautiful green gemstone emerald. However, beryl is actually a very important mineral for a whole assortment of valuable gemstones, including aquamarine and morganite. Beryl usually forms as long, hexagonal crystals, the largest and most impressive of which form in igneous rocks called pegmatites.

Emerald
The deep bluish-green
color comes from the
presence of chromium
and VANADIUM.

Watermelon tourmaline

TOURMALINE

Tourmaline is a semiprecious mineral, famous for having more color varieties than any other gemstone. Tourmaline is so colorful that crystals can often display up to four colors. It can occur in metamorphic rocks, but the most spectacular crystals of tourmaline usually form when hot fluids flow through cracks in cooling igneous rocks. Colorful crystals can then grow out of these fluids to fill up the empty rock spaces.

QUARTZ GEMSTONES

Quartz is one of the most common minerals on the planet—but it's also a valuable jewel. It is hard-wearing and occurs in a variety of colors and patterns, making it a very popular gemstone.

Quartz gems can be split into two groups: crystalline quartz and chalcedony. Crystalline quartz grows as single crystals whereas chalcedony is made from millions of tiny microscopic quartz crystals stuck together.

Opaque red jasper

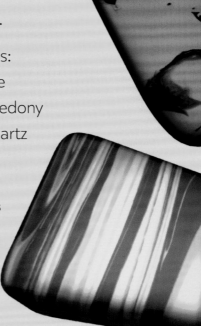

Tiger's eye

Agate

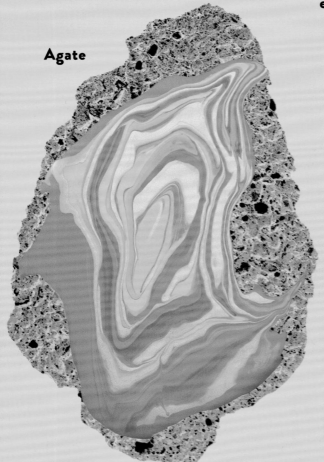

CHALCEDONY

Agate is common type of chalcedony that has an eye-catching pattern of colorful rings. This striking gemstone forms in gaps and hollows in igneous rocks. In these gaps, thin layers of chalcedony are laid down by mineral-rich waters and slowly build up into colorful, banded geodes. Other popular chalcedony gemstones are tiger's eye and jasper. Tiger's eye is easy to recognize from its pattern of golden parallel stripes that move back and forth when turned. Jasper is an opaque gemstone and commonly an earthy red color due to the presence of iron.

Rose quartz

CRYSTALLINE QUARTZ

Commonly found in geodes, amethyst is the most popular quartz gemstone. Amethyst comes in many different shades of purple, but most valuable crystals are a deep purple color. Citrine is another crystalline quartz gemstone with a rich orange color. In nature, citrine is rare and only forms when amethyst crystals are put under extreme pressures in the Earth's crust and heated to more than 930°F! Rose quartz, smoky quartz, and greeny-blue aventurine are other crystalline quartz gemstones. They get their attractive colors from the presence of other minerals and metals in their crystal structures.

Amethyst

Citrine

Smoky quartz

Aventurine

COLORFUL JEWELS

Gemstones are valued for their vibrant colors.
The shiny feldspars and the greeny-blue copper minerals
are fairly common minerals on Earth, but their striking
colors and interesting reflective patterns make them
attractive gemstones.

Moonstone

This is probably the most famous
feldspar gemstone, named after
its pearly-white shimmer that
resembles moonlight.

FELDSPAR GEMSTONES

Feldspar is the most
common mineral in the
Earth's crust.

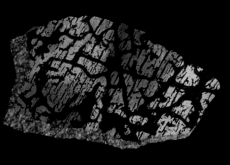

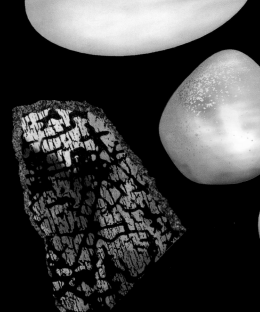

Labradorite

This is a popular feldspar
gemstone found in basalt and
gabbro rocks. It is dark bluish-gray
in color and it reflects flashes
of multicolored light, known as
IRIDESCENCE.

Sunstone and Amazonite

These are other feldspar gemstones.
Sunstone is peachy-orange in color
and often contains specks of red
COPPER. Like the rain forest it is
named after, Amazonite is a beautiful
sea-green and usually has white veins
running through it.

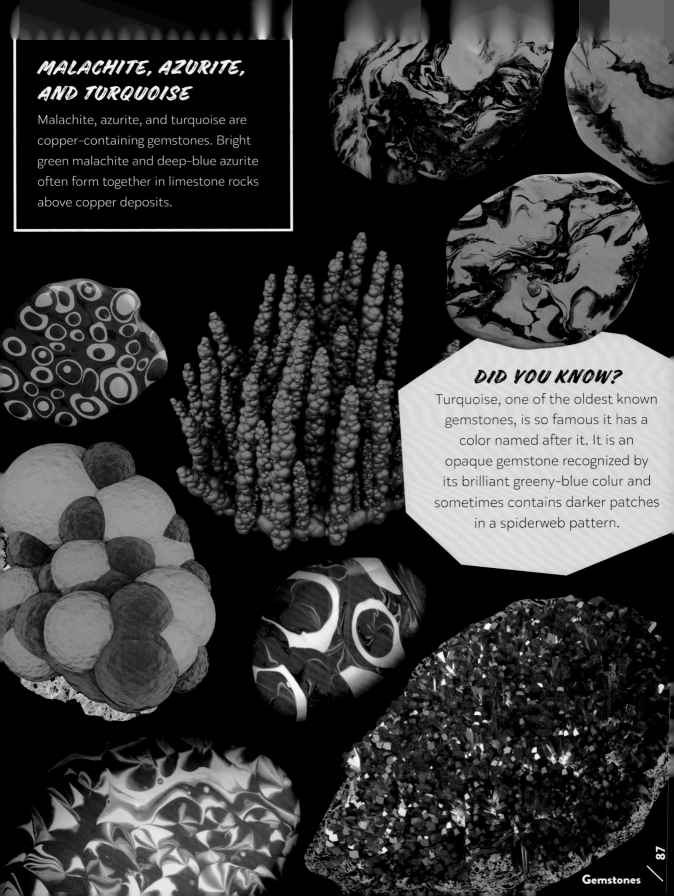

MALACHITE, AZURITE, AND TURQUOISE

Malachite, azurite, and turquoise are copper-containing gemstones. Bright green malachite and deep-blue azurite often form together in limestone rocks above copper deposits.

DID YOU KNOW?

Turquoise, one of the oldest known gemstones, is so famous it has a color named after it. It is an opaque gemstone recognized by its brilliant greeny-blue colur and sometimes contains darker patches in a spiderweb pattern.

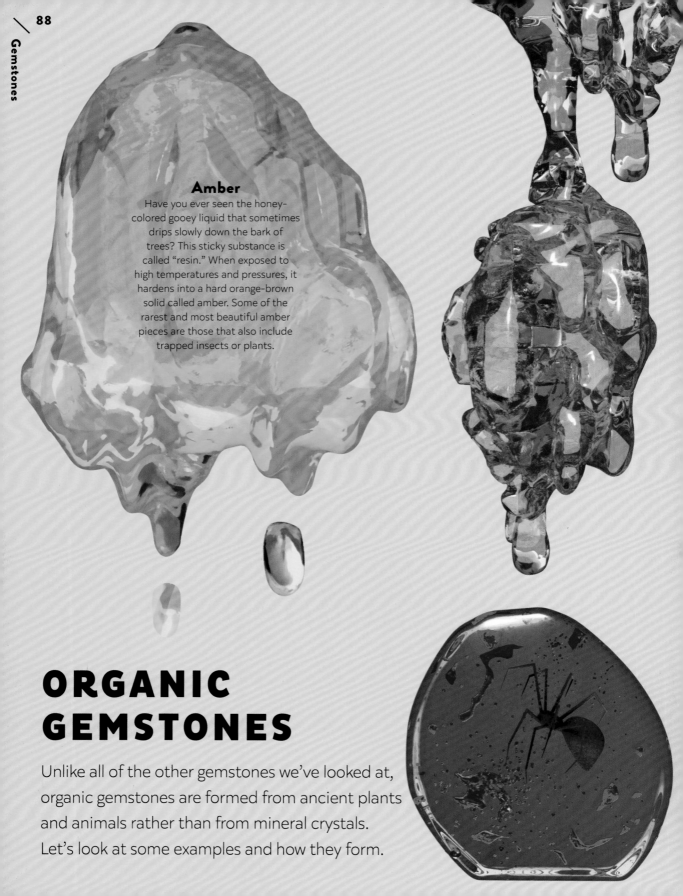

Amber

Have you ever seen the honey-colored gooey liquid that sometimes drips slowly down the bark of trees? This sticky substance is called "resin." When exposed to high temperatures and pressures, it hardens into a hard orange-brown solid called amber. Some of the rarest and most beautiful amber pieces are those that also include trapped insects or plants.

ORGANIC GEMSTONES

Unlike all of the other gemstones we've looked at, organic gemstones are formed from ancient plants and animals rather than from mineral crystals. Let's look at some examples and how they form.

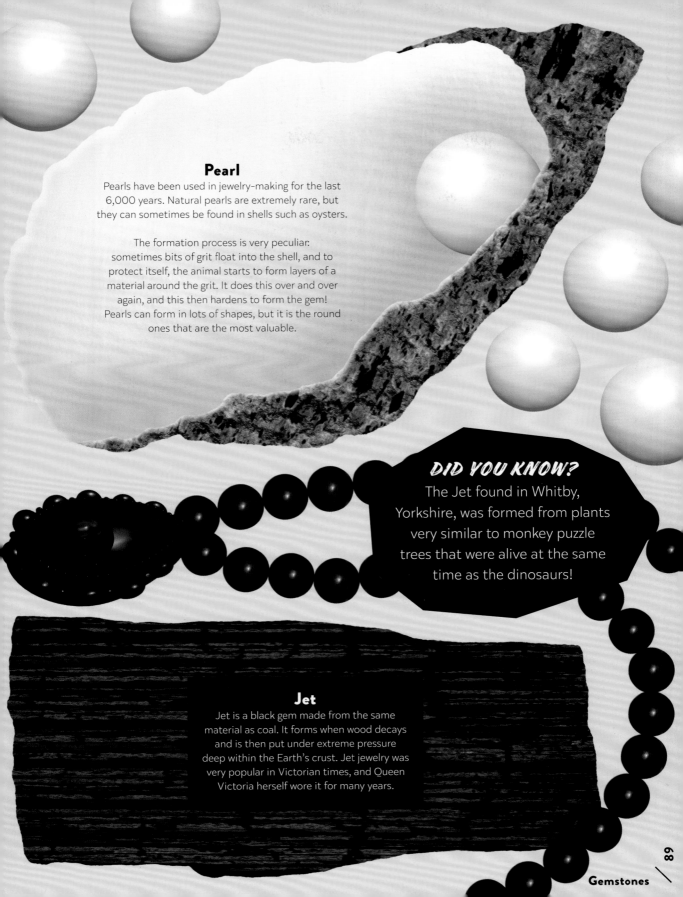

Pearl

Pearls have been used in jewelry-making for the last 6,000 years. Natural pearls are extremely rare, but they can sometimes be found in shells such as oysters.

The formation process is very peculiar: sometimes bits of grit float into the shell, and to protect itself, the animal starts to form layers of a material around the grit. It does this over and over again, and this then hardens to form the gem! Pearls can form in lots of shapes, but it is the round ones that are the most valuable.

DID YOU KNOW?

The Jet found in Whitby, Yorkshire, was formed from plants very similar to monkey puzzle trees that were alive at the same time as the dinosaurs!

Jet

Jet is a black gem made from the same material as coal. It forms when wood decays and is then put under extreme pressure deep within the Earth's crust. Jet jewelry was very popular in Victorian times, and Queen Victoria herself wore it for many years.

PRECIOUS METALS

Precious metals are ones that are valued for their pretty appearance.

Gold, silver, and platinum are some of the most prized metals. They are the least reactive metals, which is why they have been used since ancient times for jewelry and ornaments—because they don't change color or decay easily.

Gold

Gold is a very precious metal that has been used in religious traditions and jewelry-making around the world for thousands of years. It was even the foundation of the banking industry! Gold is often found on its own as nuggets, grains, or veins in other rocks.

DID YOU KNOW?

Silver is one of the earliest metals ever discovered by humans, with evidence suggesting it was used by people more than 5,000 years ago.

Silver

Silver is also used in the making of jewelry and decorative items but has uses in other items like batteries, electronics, coins, and is sometimes even woven into clothing.

DID YOU KNOW?

Most of the gold, silver, and platinum found at the Earth's surface is thought to have arrived on meteorites from outer space!

Platinum

Platinum is a silvery-gray metal that is a popular choice for wedding rings but is also used in medication and magnets. Over 80% of platinum deposits are found in South Africa.

USEFUL METALS

Not all metals are "precious metals" used in jewelry or precious objects. Many are used to produce and build the things we use in our everyday lives.

DID YOU KNOW?

Lead was used by the ancient Egyptians as makeup to darken eyelids and by the ancient Romans to make their water pipes.

Lead

Lead is used in batteries and weights for weight lifting.

Zinc

Zinc is often mixed with other metals to improve their quality and is used in making paints, soap, batteries, and medicine.

Galena

Sphalerite

Iron

Iron is used to make steel, a very important metal in the construction of buildings, bridges, railways, and many other structures.

Hematite

Lithium

Lithium is the lightest of all the metals. You can find lithium inside all of the batteries that power mobile phones, laptops, electric cars, and lots of other portable electronics.

Spodumene

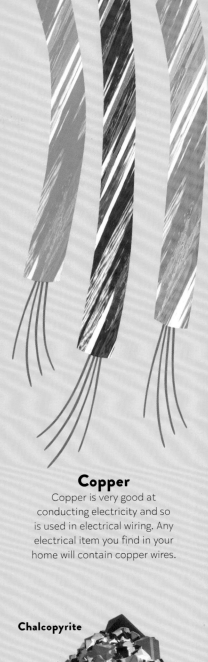

Copper

Copper is very good at conducting electricity and so is used in electrical wiring. Any electrical item you find in your home will contain copper wires.

Chalcopyrite

Gemstones

GLOSSARY

Asterism – star-shaped pattern of light that can be seen in some gemstones

Boron – a chemical element

Carat – a measurement of mass in precious gemstones

Carbon – a chemical element, found in all living things.

Chemical elements – the materials that all matter is made from, made from atoms of the same type

Chromium – a chemical element and type of metal

Clastic – rocks made up of broken pieces of other, older rocks

Copper – a chemical element and type of metal

Craton – ancient parts of continents

Crystal – a solid that is arranged in an ordered pattern.

Crystal structure – the arrangement of chemical elements in a crystal

Cycad – an ancient plant that looks like a palm tree

Evaporate – when liquids turn into gas

Feldspar – a common mineral

Fossil – remains of ancient plants and animals turned into rock

Geodes – hollow rocks that contain large crystals

Geology – the study of the Earth

Geologist – a scientist who studies the Earth

Igneous rock – rocks made from cooling molten rock

Inorganic – not made from living things like plants and animals, e.g., metal

Interglacial – a warmer time period in between two colder periods

Intergrown – crystals that grow into each other

Invertebrate – animal without a backbone

Iridescent – flashes of multicolored light that change with movement

Iron – a chemical element and type of metal

Karst – landscape made of limestone rock that has been dissolved to create features like sinkholes and towers

Kimberlite – rare igneous rocks that can contain diamonds

Lava – molten rock above the Earth's surface

Lunar highlands – the lighter surfaces on Earth's moon, which represent areas that are higher up

Lunar mare – the dark surfaces on Earth's moon, made of basalt

Lunar regolith – a layer of dust, soil, and small rocks on the surface of Earth's moon

Magma – molten rock beneath the Earth's surface

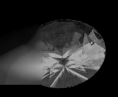
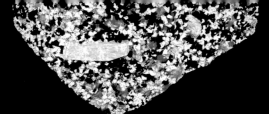
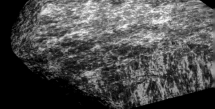

Magnesium — a chemical element and type of metal

Mantle — the layer of solid rock beneath the Earth's crust

Metamorphic rock — rocks that are changed when they are put under extreme pressure and heat

Mineral — the building blocks of rocks, such as quartz and feldspar

Nickel — a chemical element and type of metal

Nitrogen — a chemical element and type of gas

Opaque — you can't see through it

Organic — made from living things like plants and animals

Pangea — supercontinent that existed on Earth around 270 million years ago

Pegmatite — igneous rock formed under the Earth's surface, made from very large crystals

Plankton — small, microscopic organisms that live in water

Prehistoric — the time before historical records were written down

Pressure — the physical force of something pushing something else

Sedimentary rock — rocks made from bits of other rocks and the remains of plants and animals

Silica — a chemical made from the elements silicon

Silicates — minerals made from silica and other elements

Strata — layers of sedimentary rocks

Tar — a dark, sticky liquid that can be made from coal, wood, or petroleum

Tectonic plate — slabs of the Earth's surface made from the crust and upper part of the mantle

Titanium — a chemical element and type of metal

Transparent — you can see through it

Vanadium — a chemical element and type of metal

Vertebrate — animal with a backbone

Xenolith — a bit of rock trapped within another igneous rock

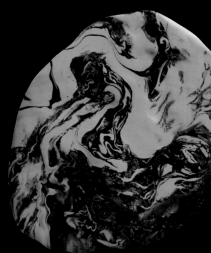

Inspiring | Educating | Creating | Entertaining

Brimming with creative inspiration, how-to projects, and useful information to enrich your everyday life, Quarto Knows is a favorite destination for those pursuing their interests and passions. Visit our site and dig deeper with our books into your area of interest: Quarto Creates, Quarto Cooks, Quarto Homes, Quarto Lives, Quarto Drives, Quarto Explores, Quarto Gifts, or Quarto Kids.

ISBN 978-1-78603-873-9
The illustrations were created digitally.
Set in Karu Light, Pluto Black, and Handelson Two.

Published by Jenny Broom and Rachel Williams
Designed by Nicola Price
Edited by Katy Flint
Production by Nicolas Zeifman

Manufactured in Guangdong, China CC052019

9 8 7 6 5 4 3 2 1